KLAUSUREN

Englisch Oberstufe

STARK

Autoren/Autorinnen:
Andrea Bailer
Silvia Berger-Hönge
Christina Diehr
Dr. Dirk Großklaus
Simon Hauzenberger
Rainer Jacob
Paul Jenkinson
Christine Netzler
Elena Nowitzki
Constantin Rieske

Umschlagbild: © Iliya Mitskavets. Fotolia.de

www.stark-verlag.de
1. Auflage 2018

Inhalt

Hördateien und Video

Track 1: Is London what it used to be?
Track 2: Digital breadcrumbs: the data trail we leave behind us
Track 3: *'Hidden Figures'* author Margot Lee Shetterly
Track 4: Fair is foul and foul is fair – Shakespeare's Macbeth
Video: Bolivia: Crazy for Quinoa

Auf die Hördateien und das Video können Sie **online** auf der Plattform **MyStark** zugreifen. Verwenden Sie dazu Ihren **persönlichen Zugangscode** auf der Umschlaginnenseite.

Autoren/Autorinnen:

Andrea Bailer/Elena Nowitzki (Klausur 7, Sprechprüfungen)
Silvia Berger-Hönge (Klausur 1 und 3)
Christina Diehr (Klausur 8 und 11)
Dr. Dirk Großklaus (Klausur 9)
Simon Hauzenberger (Klausur 4)
Rainer Jacob (Klausur 5)
Paul Jenkinson (Klausur 6)
Christine Netzler (Klausur 10)
Constantin Rieske (Klausur 2)

Vorwort

Liebe Schülerinnen und Schüler,

der vorliegende Band gibt Ihnen die Möglichkeit, sich umfassend auf **Klausuren in der Oberstufe** vorzubereiten und sich mit den typischen Aufgabenformaten vertraut zu machen. Die Themen und Aufgabenformate sowie die Kompetenzbereiche der Klausuren orientieren sich an den Lehrplänen verschiedener Bundesländer und den Bildungsstandards der Oberstufe. Dabei orientieren sich die Klausuren 1 bis 6 in diesem Buch an einem grundlegenden, die Klausuren 7 bis 11 an einem erhöhten Anforderungsniveau.

Die Klausuren bestehen **jeweils aus zwei Teilen**. Ein Teil umfasst einen Kompetenzbereich wie Leseverstehen, Hörverstehen, Hör-/Sehverstehen und Sprachmittlung. Der andere Teil („Textaufgabe“) ist, was Inhalt und Schwierigkeitsgrad angeht, komplexer, da er auch die Kompetenz Schreiben/Textproduktion beinhaltet. Hier wird Ihnen ein Text (Sachtext oder literarisch) und eventuell auch zusätzliches Material (z. B. Poster, Cartoon) vorgelegt. Die anschließenden (offenen) Aufgaben beziehen sich dann auf den Text und ggf. das Material. Sie beinhalten auch eine oft kreative Aufgabenstellung, die von Ihnen verlangt, einen eigenen Text zu verfassen.

Die **Lösungen** enthalten zusätzliche **Hinweise und Tipps**, die je nach Thema, Aufgabenformat und Schwierigkeitsgrad ausführlicher oder knapper formuliert sind. Beispiellösungen zur Textproduktion im Teil „Textaufgabe“ sollen Ihnen vor allem als Anregung dienen und möglichst viele inhaltliche Aspekte und Formulierungsmöglichkeiten aufzeigen.

Wenn eine Klausur in diesem Band den Vorgaben in Ihrem Bundesland nicht 1:1 entspricht, können Sie auch nur den Teil bearbeiten, der für Sie relevant ist. Allerdings kann es sich lohnen, auch an nicht prüfungsrelevanten Aufgabenformaten z. B. das Textverständnis zu trainieren oder die eigene Textproduktion zu verbessern.

Zusätzlich zu den schriftlichen Klausuren enthält der Band auch noch zwei Beispiele für **mündliche Prüfungen**, um Ihnen eine Orientierung zu geben, wie diese ablaufen können.

Viel Erfolg in den Klausuren und in der Prüfung wünschen Ihnen
der Verlag und das Autorenteam

Klausur 1: Social Life/Multicultural Society

Sprachmittlung 30 min.

Du bist sooo süß!!!

Cameron Dallas, 22, betreibt die totale Selbstvermarktung. Dafür lieben ihn Millionen Teenager – und die Konzerne, für die er wirbt. von Jana Gioia Baurmann

Wenn man 21 Jahre alt ist und Cameron Dallas heißt, reichen 140 Zeichen und ein Sieben-Sekunden-Video, um eine Stadt lahmzulegen.

Es war Anfang 2016, als Dallas in Mailand war, das Modehaus Calvin Klein hatte ihn zur Fashion Week eingeladen. Dazu muss man wissen, dass Cameron Dallas Millionen Fans hat, Millionen Menschen, die ihm auf Twitter, Snapchat, Instagram und vier weiteren Kanälen folgen. Das macht Cameron Dallas zu einem sogenannten Influencer, zu einem, der Einfluss hat also. Wenn jemand wie Dallas twittert, dass er im Park Hyatt in Mailand seinen Fans Hallo sagen will, kommen Tausende. […] Die Mädchen unten auf der Straße drehen durch, Dallas steht oben und winkt, man denkt an den Papst und den Petersplatz, die Größenordnung ist ähnlich. „Ich wollte Calvin Klein die Macht von Social Media zeigen", wird Dallas später in einem Interview sagen.

Das Magazin Forbes zählt Dallas zu den 30 einflussreichsten Menschen in Hollywood

Inzwischen ist Cameron Dallas 22 Jahre alt. Seit der Sache in Mailand hat er eine Welttournee mit Magcon hinter sich, einem Influencer-Kollektiv, das wie eine Boygroup vor Publikum auftritt. Magazine wie *Vogue Hommes* lichteten Dallas ab, Marken wie American Eagle und Hollister werben mit seinem Gesicht. Ende Dezember gab die amerikanische Burger-Kette Umami bekannt, dass es ab sofort den „Cameron Dallas BBQBurger" zu kaufen gibt. Etwa zeitgleich erschien auf Netflix eine Doku-Serie mit und über ihn, *Chasing Cameron* heißt die, er hat sie praktischerweise auch gleich mit produziert. Die Zuschauer erleben den Aufstieg von Cameron Dallas und sind bei der Welttournee von Magcon dabei. Und glaubt man dem amerikanischen Magazin *Forbes*, zählt Cameron Dallas seit vergangener Woche zu den 30 einflussreichsten Menschen unter 30 in Hollywood. […]

Influencer wie Cameron Dallas können vor allem eines gut: sich selbst darstellen. […] Anders als früher, als Models, Sänger oder Schauspieler entdeckt und dann im besten Fall berühmt wurden, hat sich Cameron Dallas um alles selbst gekümmert. Mehr *self-made man* geht nicht. Den Anfang seiner Karriere begründeten kein Modelscout und kein Plattenlabel, keine Castings oder irgendwelche Treffen mit Managern. „Ich habe angefangen, mich selbst als Model zu vermarkten", sagt Cameron Dallas in der Serie. 2011 twitterte er: "I want to be a Calvin Klein Model". Heute, fünf Jahre später, setzt ihn das Modelabel bei der Fashion Week nicht nur in die erste Reihe, es startete auch eine Werbekampagne mit Dallas. […]

Mit seinen Followern scheint Dallas alles zu teilen: […] Man weiß, wann Dallas unreine Haut hat und wann er beim Friseur war.

Das hört sich banal an, ist aber knallhartes Business. Denn Cameron Dallas teilt nicht nur mit, dass „light brown“ nun seine neue Haarfarbe ist, er analysiert auch, wie diese Meldung bei den Followern ankommt. Wie viele Likes gibt es und in welcher Zeit die meisten? Wie oft wird das Foto geteilt? Wie oft wird es kommentiert? Die Follower sehen Bauchmuskeln und Spiegel-Selfies von ihrem Idol, Dallas sieht Balken, Tortendiagramme und Graphen. […] Seine Mutter nennt ihn „business-wise“.

Weil Cameron Dallas gefühlt 99,9 Prozent seines Lebens teilt, baut er eine extrem enge Bindung zu seinen Fans auf. Parasoziale Beziehung nennt man das: Die Fans meinen, ihr Idol zu kennen, ihm nah zu sein. Und anders als bei Models, Schauspielern oder Sängern geht es bei Influencern auch wirklich darum, die Fans zu treffen. Wenige Sekunden Video oder ein Tweet reichen, um den Treffpunkt durchzugeben. […]

Schaut man sich die Auftritte an, wird klar, dass weder Dallas noch die Fans Distanz kennen. Wie am Fließband sagt Dallas „I love you!“, fürs Foto küsst er Mädchen auf die Wange, umarmt sie wie enge Freundinnen. Die Fans wiederum fassen Dallas einfach an, wollen, dass er sie auf Händen trägt, manche bespringen ihn auch einfach. Und sie geben Regieanweisungen fürs perfekte Bild: „Können wir Händchen halten, während du meine Stirn küsst?“, sagt ein Mädchen […]. Es ist mehr Befehl als Frage. „Okay“, antwortet Cameron Dallas. […] *(640 Wörter)*

Annotation

l. 15 Magcon Abkürzung für „Meet and Greet Convention“

Task

Point out how Cameron Dallas influences his followers. *(30)*

Textaufgabe 90 min.

Text: A British Muslim girl about to make a decision

Shanaz was a year into her A-levels when she noticed that her mother had started buying the kind of things that normally presage a wedding. […] “We are going to Pakistan,” her mother would say by way of explanation. Shanaz did not need to ask why to know that her life was about to be rearranged.

The subject of her marriage had been in the air ever since she was into her teens. “My mother would have been happy if I’d stopped school at twelve,” she told me as we walked along the lake at Lister Park on a sunny but windy late spring day. The final decision about her education was settled in the intimacy of a family chat, but by a group of elders, all men. “I think there were about twelve of them,” she said. Her father had told the other men that Shanaz was keen to go on to university. They were opposed to the idea, portraying university life as licentious and unsuitable for a Muslim girl. They might have found the bitter pill easier to swallow if Shanaz had wanted to study something that could be useful to the community but she wanted to take art. […]

It is a tribute to Shanaz's determination that the elders eventually relented. She was allowed to continue her A-level course and apply for a place at university though there was what Shanaz called an "indirect" condition that marriage would be thrown into the bargain – no dates, just a commitment. When I first met her, Shanaz's hair was dyed red with a lightning streak of silver-grey that swept back from her forehead – a work of art in itself. To see her is to wonder why a woman of such independence, such verve, could ever have countenanced wedlock at a time other than that of her own choosing and to a man she did not know.

The only way she could explain her acquiescence was simple but, as we shall see, tragic: "I went to Pakistan because I loved my parents. I never did love my partner, but I did love my mother and father. I did it for them."

The man chosen as her husband was a first cousin back in Mirpur. Ali Shezad […] was a year older than his bride-to-be but light years behind her in education, aspiration and outlook. Shanaz, even if she was brought up within the confines of a Muslim home, was a child of the city, a British city at that. She is a living embodiment of all the contradictions that swirl around the lives of so many young immigrants: Asian but British; a woman but independent; a Muslim but with secular values; above all a dutiful daughter but with a sense of her own being. Her husband-to-be had the customs and traditions of Mirpur written into his bones. […] If in her mind Shanaz had decided to accept her place in the family plan, the same could not be said of her heart. Within days of getting to Pakistan, she fell ill, losing all her hair and dropping down to five stone in weight. And still the wedding took place – the honour of the *biradari* apparently more important than the health of an individual. *(548 words)*

Annotation

l. 35 biradari word of Persian origin meaning "brotherhood"; it can be described as a particular group descended of the same ancestor, with its individuals sharing common characteristics and being emotionally linked with it

Material: Poster

FMU, Open Government Licence v3.0

Tasks

1. Sum up the text in your own words. *(15)*
2. Relate Shanaz' situation to the message conveyed through the poster. *(25)*
3. Comment on the decision Shanaz made about her marriage, taking into account possible developments in the future. *(30)*

Lösungsvorschläge

Sprachmittlung

Hinweis: *How to approach the task:*
Step 1: Read the text carefully and highlight how Cameron Dallas exerts influence.
Step 2: Start off with an "umbrella sentence" containing the source and the topic.
Step 3: Omit minor details and write a maximum of 200 words.

The article from *Die Zeit* deals with Cameron Dallas, a 22-year-old model, who is able to influence millions of followers via social media and is considered to be among the thirty most influential people under 30 in Hollywood. Whenever Cameron twitters that he will appear somewhere to greet his fans, thousands of people come to see him, and girls go crazy.
Together with a collective of influencers, Cameron Dallas has completed a world tour in a similar way to a boy group. His photographs appear in magazines and advertisements. Not only has an American hamburger chain named a special burger after him, but Dallas is also a co-producer of a documentary about his own life.
The key to Cameron's success is his professional self-marketing, which basically consists of sharing his private life on social media and then analysing the likes and comments. This leads to a parasocial connection with his fans, who believe that they are close to their idol. A short video or tweet mobilises them to meet, kiss and hug him.

(173 words)

Textaufgabe

1. ***Hinweis:*** *How to approach the task:*
   Step 1: Read the text carefully and underline the facts concerning Shanaz' arranged marriage.
   Step 2: Start off with an "umbrella sentence" including the source and the topic.
   Step 3: Limit yourself to a maximum of 220 words.

   The extract from "A Home from Home" by George Alagiah deals with a British Muslim girl who gives in to a marriage arranged by her family although she would like to study art at university.
   Shanaz' mother, who would have liked her daughter to quit school at the age of twelve, started preparing for the wedding before the final decision was made by a group of elderly men in the family clan. They were opposed to university, since they considered this an unsuitable and tempting environment for a Muslim girl. Nevertheless, Shanaz was allowed to graduate from school and apply to university in return for agreeing to the arranged marriage.
   Shanaz, who is described as a modern and independent girl with a secular outlook, finally ends up in Pakistan married to a first cousin from a traditional, less educated,

rural background. She has agreed to get married out of love for her parents, yet she is heartbroken and seriously ill because she had to give up her aspirations.

(168 words)

2. ***Hinweis:*** *How to approach the task:*
Step 1: Consider that Shanaz agreed to the arranged marriage because she was under pressure from her family.
Step 2: Look at the poster carefully and consider the visual elements as well as the text.
Step 3: Establish a connection to Shanaz' life.

The poster, which was published by the UK government, consists of two parts which stand in contrast to each other. On the left, you can see a wedding ring and the message that marriage should be based on choice. On the right, which is much darker, the ring has been turned into a chain and the caption stresses that forced marriage is a crime. This discrepancy between personal choice and external pressure or force is quite similar to Shanaz' dilemma.

Shanaz is torn between the aspirations of a modern girl living in a western country and the expectations of her traditional Pakistani family, who want her to marry young and who decide on her husband. In the western world, however, being forced into marriage is considered an infringement of personal liberty. In the government campaign poster, women who are affected are encouraged to contact the Forced Marriage Unit to seek help.

Yet Shanaz, who is depicted as a modern and urban woman with secular values, gives in to her parents' wishes because she loves them and does not want to disappoint them. In the end, tradition and family ties were stronger than her personal happiness, and she agreed to marry her first cousin, whom she does not love. This can easily be related to the chain on the right-hand side of the poster, since the effects are quite similar. Shanaz is now chained to a husband she did not choose herself and with whom she has nothing in common. The discrepancy between western individualism and traditional family values makes Shanaz seriously ill after moving to Pakistan.

The British government, which published the campaign poster, regards forced marriage as a crime and a violation of individual rights. For traditional Muslims, however, the honour of the family is considered more important. It is astonishing that a modern girl like Shanaz, who grew up in England, should give in to her parents' wishes without being explicitly forced to do so. Perhaps if she had seen the poster, she might have resisted an arranged marriage. Nevertheless, if marriages are forced upon minors, this is certainly a violation of human rights. *(356 words)*

3. ***Hinweis:*** *How to approach the task:*
Step 1: Keep in mind that Shanaz was pressured into marrying her cousin in Pakistan and that she is suffering from the consequences.
Step 2: Imagine what her future life could be like and take a stand.

The marriage is not likely to be happy. Shanaz and her husband are fundamentally different because of the cultural divide between them as far as world view, level of education and religion are concerned. This would make it hard for the couple to get close to each other.
If Shanaz recovers and stays in Pakistan, she might adapt to the expectations of her traditional surroundings and give up her own plans and aspirations. She may have many children and she will be confined to the house. Additionally, she will be dependent on her husband and his clan, who will expect her to cast off the individualism which was once part of her personality. On the one hand, Shanaz might eventually get used to her new role, but on the other hand, she is in danger of becoming unhappy for the rest of her life.
Shanaz might return to England with her husband and family. This could cause difficulties, since her husband is less qualified and probably does not speak English well or at all. If Shanaz is lucky, she might become the breadwinner of the family on condition that her husband allows her to complete her studies and go to work. If he does not, there will certainly be financial problems in addition to the cultural tensions. Yet, to a certain extent her husband would have to adapt to the new host culture. Whether their marriage will succeed, depends on his potential for personal and professional development. From the text, we can assume that coping with western society would be a fundamental challenge for him.
All in all, I consider Shanaz' decision to marry her cousin a great mistake, and her bad health just after arriving in Pakistan shows that she is suffering. From a western point of view, it is hard to understand why she made such a sacrifice. Of course she loves her parents, but she is still an individual human being with a right to be happy. Moreover, Shanaz should have developed a stronger will or should at least have tried to convince her parents that education and a career are important for girls as well as for boys. She obviously avoided a conflict with her family. At the same time, she has risked her future and her health. *(382 words)*

Klausur 2: Science and Technology

Sprachmittlung 45 min.

Forschung an der Zukunftsmaschine: Die Berechnung der Welt

Die Finanzkrise hätte es nicht gegeben, der Tsunami hätte nicht 230.000 Menschen getötet, und auch Hitler wäre nicht an die Macht gekommen: Wenn alles nur besser gesteuert wäre. Dirk Helbing läuft mit großen Schritten auf das sozialwissenschaftliche Institut der Eidgenössischen Technischen Hochschule in Zürich zu. Der Professor hat es eilig. Er will die Zivilisation retten. Mit Computern, die den Menschen helfen, sich selbst zu steuern. […] So soll die Zukunft vorhersehbar werden.

„Wir verstehen die Zusammenhänge in der globalisierten Welt nicht mehr gut genug", sagt Helbing. Unsere Gehirne hätten Mühe, das Zusammenspiel des Handelns vieler Akteure zu verstehen. Ihm sei klar geworden: Die Zeit ist reif für sein Projekt zur Berechnung der Welt. „FuturICT", was, entknotet und ins Deutsche übersetzt, ungefähr bedeutet: die Vorhersage der Zukunft mit Informations- und Kommunikationstechnik. Was die Gehirne der Politiker nicht leisten können, müsse die Technik erledigen. „Wir brauchen neue Erkenntnisinstrumente. Früher gab es ein Fernrohr, in Zukunft muss es Instrumente geben, die Feedback- und Kaskadeneffekte im Vorfeld erkennen lassen." […] Gerade in der globalisierten Welt könnte die Gefahr von Kettenreaktionen wachsen. Wie in der Physik, fand er, müsste man die zugrunde liegenden Gesetze erkennen, um solche Krisen vorherzusehen und abzuwenden.

Zuerst hat sich Helbing Fußgänger angeschaut – bei denen funktioniere alles reibungslos: Fußgänger überholen sich, laufen aneinander vorbei oder nebeneinander her, ohne sich gegenseitig zu behindern. Sie bahnen sich ihren Weg, trotz Gegenverkehr, trotz unterschiedlicher Geschwindigkeiten. Auf Konferenzen zeigt Helbing Videoaufnahmen von Fußgängerzonen. „Sehen Sie", sagt er dabei, „von ganz allein machen Passantenkollektive alles richtig. Da klappt die Selbststeuerung!" Warum klappt sie aber nicht bei Autofahrern, die Staus verursachen, bei Fans der Loveparade, die sich in einen Tunnel drängten, bei Feueralarm im Kaufhaus oder bei Pilgern in Mekka? „Das Problem ist hierbei immer, dass das Ergebnis der Interaktion etwas ist, das keiner will. Selbstorganisation funktioniert bei diesen Kollektiven nicht." […] In Zusammenarbeit mit Verkehrsplanern und Behörden hat er die Sicherheit der Pilgerrituale in Mekka erhöht. Die Trophäe, die seine Leistung in arabischen Schriftzügen würdigt, steht auf dem Regal neben dem Schreibtisch.

Während er die Interaktion der Pilger von Mekka vorausberechnet hat, will er den Verkehr in Echtzeit programmieren. Auf einer Konferenz in Berlin im August präsentierte er mit einer Computersimulation, wie es zu Stau auf der Autobahn kommt. „Dieses Auto", er deutete auf einen schnellen roten Sportwagen, „müsste nur ein bisschen langsamer fahren." Seine Simulation zeigt: Stau entsteht, weil Autofahrer keinen Überblick haben. „Wird die Interaktion aber leicht geändert, funktioniert alles störungsfrei!"

Aber wie soll die Interaktion geändert werden? Will Helbing die Autos alle mit einem Supercomputer verbinden, der sie entsprechend seinen Berechnungen fernsteuert? „Nein", wehrt Helbing ab, „wir wollen keinen Big-Brother-Apparat entwerfen." Zusammen mit Volkswagen hat er computergestützte Assistenten für Fahrzeuge entwickelt. Sie kommunizieren miteinander und geben den Fahrern Ratschläge zur Geschwindigkeit. So braucht es keine Zentrale wie den Radiosender und seine Verkehrsmeldungen mehr. […] Auch Ampeln programmiert er so, dass sie je nach Verkehr die Farbe wechseln. Darauf hat er ein Patent. „Verkehrsströme sollen die Ampeln steuern und nicht andersherum, der wohlmeinende Diktator funktioniert nicht. Die Komplexität der Welt kann nur mit mehr Dezentralität bewältigt werden." […]

Der Glaube daran, neue technische Instrumente seien per se emanzipatorisch, sitzt tief, der Hype um die Beteiligungsmöglichkeiten des Web 2.0 hält an, und auch die „angeleitete Selbstorganisation" der Gesellschaft, die Helbing und seinem Team vorschwebt, ist nur zeitgemäß: Wenn eine Gesellschaft „sich selbst" organisiert, ist das die beste, weil natürlichste Form des Zusammenlebens – und damit diese Natur effizient ist, muss man ihr technisch auf die Sprünge helfen. *(591 Wörter)*

Task

Your school participates in an international essay competition for young adults, *A better future? – Visions for the 22nd century*.

In the semifinal, your task is to write a blog entry on a science topic of your choice. You have come across the newspaper article on "FuturICT". You decide to write a blog entry in which you summarise the main idea of "FuturICT" and describe how everyday life could be improved by it. *(30)*

Textaufgabe 90 min.

Soon robots could be taking your job interview

by Zoë Apostolides

Robots have already been put to work across a number of industries. They are manufacturing cars, taking care of the elderly, doing housework, homework, and even entering literary awards. It is not surprising then that new robots have been developed to conduct job interviews.

One such robot, Matlda, has been programmed to conduct 25-minute interviews in which she works through a roster of up to 76 questions. She records and analyses the interviewee's responses, monitors facial expressions and compares them to other successful employees within the hiring company.

Matlda is not much taller than a wine bottle, but her introduction could set a new precedent for recruitment techniques across a range of sectors.

Doing so will affect the performance of interviewees differently. "Some candidates might present better in person and will be left worse off, but others may be more comfortable with a remote interview," says Martin Ford, an expert on automation technology.

One particular demographic that might welcome chatting to Matlda is the post-millennial generation, also known as digital natives, who grew up swiping the pages of digital books, using self-checkout machines and asking Siri for directions. "We find that people often prefer to interact with something that's not real; it's all about reducing the cognitive load," says Matthew Howard at King's College London, whose students launched Kinba, a robotic receptionist at the university, earlier this year.

As with all forms of artificial intelligence, efficiency is a clear incentive. More important, though, are claims that artificial intelligence will help eliminate pre-existing prejudice within employment processes and boost transparency.

"Matlda's mission is to be a service gateway for a more sustainable and humane society," says Prof Rajiv Khosla at Melbourne's La Trobe University, which developed the robot. "It's a non-judgmental, non-threatening and non-invasive means of engaging people in uninhibited interaction." [...]

The main advantage of involving computers, "is a consistency in decision-making and the removal of some human error", says Benedict O'Donovan, managing director at Durham Applied Robotics and Technologies. "While you might get two interviewers who interpret recruiting guidelines very differently, you're never going to get a computer that doesn't follow the rules exactly or allow prejudice to bias their decisions."

Hiring processes, when conducted by humans at least, have always been problematic because bias is so often unconscious. Personality and psychometric testing, blind auditions, webcam interviews and nameless CVs are on the rise, but in a face-to-face environment, anything from gender, race, clothing, education and accent can provide an unwitting platform for discrimination. Humans are inconsistent where robots are incapable of being anything but consistent.

The problem is that as well as putting these robots to work, humans are also the ones inputting the data enabling them to do that work. "There is no such thing as a neutral algorithm," says Laurel Riek, associate professor of computer science and engineering at University of California, San Diego. "If the system is using some metric for decision-making regarding employment, who came up with that metric, what data is it based on, and how is it being applied?"

This problem was highlighted earlier in 2016 when Microsoft was forced to take its AI chatbot Tay off Twitter just hours after its launch. Robots learn from the humans they are programmed by, followed by those they interact with; it wasn't long before Tay assimilated the conversations and opinions of those around her and posted a series of racist, sexist tweets and denied the holocaust.

"Bias can creep in very easily with learning systems, and depends entirely on the data they've been trained on," says Prof Noel Sharkey at Sheffield University. This means if an organisation is already an old boys' network of employees from similar socio-economic and educational backgrounds, a robot instilled with the existing blueprint of that workforce cannot hope to make much of a diversifying impact. So despite all good intentions, it seems unlikely that robots like Matlda will become commonplace in the interview room. We may be more biased, but until a robot is able to adjust its thinking regardless of the programming it's received – itself a contradiction in terms – the most important kind of interaction will have to remain human. *(701 words)*

Tasks

1. Outline the functions of robots as presented in the article. *(10)*

2. Examine the advantages and disadvantages of robots that conduct job interviews as stated in the article. *(15)*

3. Your school participates in the international youth competition *Our world – our future*. Your task is as follows:

   "Job interviews conducted by robots: Progress or nightmare?" –
   Take a stand on this statement, also taking into account Zoë Apostolides' article and her conclusion. *(20)*

Sprachmittlung

Hinweis: *The mediation task requires you to write a blog entry in English about a German newspaper article dealing with the science project "FuturICT". First, read the task carefully, paying special attention to the communicative context. In this case, you are supposed to convey the content of the newspaper article to young adults. Therefore, it is not necessary to write in an academic style. Nevertheless, your blog entry is your school's contribution for the essay competition, so it should be written in a neutral and sophisticated style. After having read the article thoroughly, mark its structure and take some notes on the content you want to convey. When writing your text, make sure you restrict yourself to the gist of the original. Leave out unnecessary details, do not quote from the original text and do not comment on it. Use your own words rather than translating what the author of the original text said. Also, use linking words. Your text should start with an interesting introduction leading to your topic.*

FuturICT – Calculating the future for a better life

Does not every scientist work to create a better future for coming generations? Does not every scientist strive to save the world with ground-breaking inventions? The Swiss project "FuturICT" certainly thinks that big.
Professor Dirk Helbing and his team are working on participatory computing for the complex world we live in. They use the latest information and communication technology to predict the future and thus offer people the chance to make the right decisions before events happen. In a rapidly changing and complex globalised world, the everyday interactions of various participants are more intertwined than ever. Both decision makers, such as political leaders, and citizens need to rely on the latest technologies in order to make the right choices and prevent fatal chain reactions.
For starters, Helbing and his team have tried to improve the flow of traffic. Studies show that the flow of pedestrians, e. g. in pedestrian zones, works without interruption while traffic jams in cities or on motorways are a daily nuisance. The self-monitoring of large groups of pedestrians seems to work, whereas other collectives need more regulation for better flow. Thus, Helbing suggests changing the interaction of the collectives' participants with the help of computer based car assistants and smart traffic signals, for example. The car assistants communicate with each other, helping drivers to regulate their speed to ensure a smooth traffic flow. Smart traffic signals use real-time data and automated algorithms to keep the traffic flowing. In the end, the collective of car drivers profits from the regulated interaction with the help of computers and software.
The project's vision for the future is not to create the perfect super computer that is able to regulate every aspect of our lives. Instead, Helbing and his team believe that a self-organised society would be the most advanced form of human co-existence – even if it needs a bit of technological support to work efficiently. *(324 words)*

Textaufgabe

1. ***Hinweis:*** *This task requires you to outline the functions of robots as described in the article. You are required to focus only on the main aspects of the text, omitting minor details. Be as precise as possible. Structure your text well before you start to write. Do not include your own ideas, or quotes from the article. Make sure you use your own words. Your answer should contain the following aspects:*
Robots …
– *now can conduct job interviews,*
– *record and analyse the interviewee's responses,*
– *compare the collected data to find the best-fitting job applicant.*

In her article "Soon robots could be taking your job interview", published by *The Guardian*, Zoë Apostolides reports on the many functions of robots in daily life in the 21st century. Robots have already taken over a number of jobs, such as the manufacturing of cars, helping in the house, or even taking care of older people. However, Apostolides focuses on robots that have recently been developed to conduct job interviews. Matlda is one of these robots. It can record and analyse up to 76 responses of the different interviewees to her questions. Matlda is also able to scan the facial expressions of the applicants during their interview. During and after the interview, the robot compares the collected data to other successful employees within the hiring company in order to draw conclusions about which applicant could be chosen. *(138 words)*

2. ***Hinweis:*** *Describe the advantages and disadvantages of robots conducting job interviews before you give further explanation. You should also deal with the different aspects one at a time. In your answer you should refer to and quote from the article to underline your description as well as your explanation. However, avoid quoting too much as this will distract the reader from your train of thought. Your answer should contain the following aspects:*
Advantages of job interviews conducted by robots:
– *efficiency of robots,*
– *some interviewees less stressed when talking to a robot instead of a human being,*
– *no human error*
– *robots more consistent in making decisions as they are not biased towards job applicants*
Disadvantages of job interviews conducted by robots:
– *algorithms programmed by humans = robots as biased as their programmers*
– *robots learn from interaction: leading to a very homogenous choice of suitable job applicants*

In her article, the author points out several advantages and disadvantages of robots that conduct job interviews.

One major advantage of Matlda and other robots that conduct job interviews is their efficiency. Matlda, for example, can conduct 25-minute interviews asking up to 76 questions (ll. 5/6). Thus, the robot is faster than any human interviewer could be. Furthermore, Matlda makes interviewees who tend to get nervous when faced with a real person feel more comfortable. "Digital natives", in particular, may prefer being interviewed by a machine as they have always been familiar with artificial intelligence (ll. 15–17). In that sense, Matlda is just another handy device like Siri on the smartphone or a self-checkout machine. However, the biggest advantage is the "consistency in decision-making and the removal of some human error", meaning the robot, unlike a human, makes no mistakes (ll. 28/29). It follows its programmed rules and therefore its decisions are not influenced by prejudice (ll. 31–33). While human beings are often affected by the interviewee's appearance, look and habitus, Matlda remains non-judgemental. It does not discriminate against the applicant due to unconscious bias, and makes consistent decisions based on its algorithm.

Yet, it is the algorithm of the robots which is their biggest disadvantage. According to experts, there is no "neutral algorithm" (l. 42), meaning that even artificial intelligence can be just as biased in its decisions as human beings. Since robots are programmed by people and thus learn from them, it is human prejudice and bias that "creep in very easily with learning systems" (l. 51). Additionally, artificial intelligence tends to adapt to the people it interacts with, just like the AI chatbot Tay, which learned racist and sexist tweets from the interactions with its Twitter followers. In Matlda's case, the robot could choose candidates that are most akin to its programmed preferences. With each new interviewee, the algorithm would confirm itself, which would ultimately lead to the pick of future employees being homogenous. Apart from potential discrimination in the process, any positive effect of a diversified workforce could be lost.

Concluding, it can be said that the use of artificial intelligence in job interviews might lead to a less biased choice of employees. Nevertheless, human interaction will still be an essential part of the process, as robots can only conduct the interviews based on the inconsistent and often biased standards of their programmers.

(401 words)

3. ***Hinweis:*** *Here, you are asked to give your own opinion on the question of whether job interviews conducted by robots constitute progress or more of a nightmare. In order to take a stand, you should draw from the information given in the article but not quote from it. Keep in mind that your text addresses young adults, as you are taking part in an international youth competition, so the style of your answer should not be too academic. However, use precise vocabulary and well-structured phrases that show your point of view. Before writing your article, decide on the aspects you may want to consider. Keep in mind that your arguments need to be relevant, plausible and not too detailed. Your text should also include an interesting introduction.*

"Job interviews conducted by robots: Progress or nightmare?"

This is an intriguing question. At first glance it would seem to be an improvement if robots conducted job interviews. Robots are certainly more effective and faster than human interviewers. They do not get exhausted and still perform well after a whole day of interviews. The cost of job interviews can also be reduced, which may sound attractive to companies. Nevertheless, the robots need constant technological maintenance, which requires extra staff, leading to an increase in operational costs. Maybe robots do not save the companies a lot of money after all.

I am also sceptical about the idea that candidates who are digital natives might prefer talking to a robot instead of a human being. I can imagine that some people might feel more comfortable sitting in front of a robot, but are these really the kind of colleagues you would want to work with on a daily basis? After all, most companies look for empathetic, open-minded and self-confident staff that are able to communicate with customers, for example. I really doubt that people who prefer talking to robots could meet these expectations. Moreover, nervous candidates could feel much more comfortable when being interviewed by a human being. Job interviews are stressful situations in which applicants should be able to perform at their best. An experienced and sensitive job interviewer could support the interviewee by putting him or her at ease through a change of protocol or an adjustment to the set of interview questions, or simply by offering a cup of tea. A robot would certainly lack both the skill to recognise nervousness and react to it. With a robot, the situation might remain uncomfortable for the applicant or might even get worse. I would argue that a robot, which is unable to be flexible and sensitive, would unintentionally discriminate against the applicant.

This leads me to my next point. The use of robots in job interviews can also be seen as progressive because the machines do not make human errors as they do not judge a person by his or her appearance, accent or skin colour. The robot simply follows the recruiting guidelines which have been programmed on its hardware. So there is no prejudice and bias in job interviews, which might result in better chances for candidates and a more heterogeneous workforce. This sounds very promising, but it does not concur with reality. Robots can be just as biased as humans, because they are programmed by humans. So there is even human bias in job interviews that are completely conducted by robots. In the end, robots just pick the applicants that their programmers want. It could be argued that this is always part of the application process, as companies always prefer a specific set of employees. Not every job applicant is perfect for the position and a tough selection process is a crucial part of recruitment. As this is true, prejudices and bias should not limit the chances of applicants. Therefore, technological support could be beneficial when assessing applicants. Robots might be of valuable assistance in this part of the application process. Yet, the robot's performance has to be monitored closely by humans in order to guarantee a fair job application procedure.

Robots conducting job interviews might seem unusual at first, but they do not have to be a nightmare if used in a sensible way. As it seems unlikely that human errors will be avoided completely by robots, the use of robots in job interviews cannot be a solution to that problem anytime in the near future. In my opinion, it is more important for companies to critically review and reflect on their criteria and methods of recruiting. In the following step, they could think about the potential use of artificial intelligence in order to improve their job interviews. *(641 words)*

Klausur 3: South Africa/The Individual and Society

Textaufgabe 90 min.

Text: Welcome to Kleinfontein, lingering outpost of apartheid South Africa

Aspiring Afrikaner-only enclaves highlight how race still shapes the nation's landscape

by Sudarsan Raghavan

At the entrance to the rural settlement of Kleinfontein is a well-kept shrine to the primary architect of apartheid. Nearby rests an old wheelbarrow, a symbol of the white Afrikaners who once ruled the country. Inside the coffee shop, at the bank, everywhere, there are only white faces. A white security guard, wearing grey camouflage, checks cars at a gate on the main road. Race is a key factor for entry. No blacks are allowed to buy or rent houses. […]

To blacks, Kleinfontein is a remnant of a painful past, a gated community of whites determined to perpetuate racist, apartheid-era practices. The several hundred whites who live there say they need to safeguard their Dutch-based Afrikaner culture and language and seek refuge from affirmative action policies and high crime rates that they blame on blacks. They insist that they are not racist, noting that they don't welcome Jews, Catholics or any English speakers, either.

Under apartheid, the white Afrikaner-led government forced blacks to live in homelands to separate the races. Today, the residents of Kleinfontein say the creation of Afrikaner homelands is the best way for South Africa to progress under the black-led government of the ruling African National Congress party.

"I am here because outside there's no place any more for us. We don't feel welcome," said Dries Oncke, 57, a resident. "That's why we start places like this and build them up. We know as Afrikaners we can be safe here. We have a place where we can be ourselves."

There are three criteria for living in Kleinfontein: residents must speak the Afrikaans language, be Protestant Christians and be descendants of the Voortrekkers, the Dutch settlers who left the British Cape Colony in the early 1800s and migrated to the interior of what is now South Africa. They came to be known as Afrikaners.

The tension over Kleinfontein and other aspiring whites-only enclaves in a country that is nearly 80 % black also reflects a broader societal conflict pitting individual rights against a community's rights. South Africa's constitution gives communities the right of cultural self-determination but also enshrines basic human rights that outlaw exclusionary practices.

"As Afrikaners, as a cultural group, we are basically a white people, a Caucasian people because of our history," said Marisa Haasbroek, a spokeswoman for the co-operative that runs the settlement. "Culturally, we are different from other people in this country, and we just want to protect our identity, and that includes language."

Local black leaders say Kleinfontein must be dismantled. Kgosientso Ramokgopa, the executive mayor of Tshwane, a municipality that includes Pretoria, the country's administrative capital, Kleinfontein and other surrounding areas, said there are "remnants of the bigger population who still think apartheid was the best system of governance, separate development premised on race".

"These are people who are still living in the past," he said, referring to the residents of Kleinfontein. "It's about time they begin to embrace the new South Africa." [...]

(493 words)

Material: Cartoon

Tasks

1. Point out what we get to know about the gated community Kleinfontein. *(15)*
2. Examine the views on present-day South Africa provided by both the article and the cartoon. *(30)*
3. Discuss whether or not the South African government should allow gated communities like Kleinfontein. *(25)*

Sprachmittlung 30 min.

Sicherheit durch Zäune? Gated Communities in Deutschland

Renate Belle ist Anfang siebzig, Rentnerin. Die gebürtige Berlinerin lebt seit elf Jahren in der Wohnanlage Arcadia, der ersten Gated Community in Deutschland. Besucher werden von Renate Belle persönlich beim Pförtner abgeholt. Mit entschiedenem Schritt führt die kleine Dame durch die Wohnanlage. Auf den ersten Blick wirkt die Arcadia wie ein Feriendorf: angelegte Beete, gestutzte Hecken. Dazwischen die sandfarbenen Mehrfamilienhäuser mit Balkon oder Terrasse.

Die Dreizimmerwohnung von Renate Belle ist komfortabel. Das gute Gefühl lassen sich die Bewohner einiges kosten: Fast 800 Euro zahlt Renate Belle monatlich. Dafür bekommt sie das Komplettpaket: Sicherheitszaun und Überwachungskameras. Ein Tiefgaragenstellplatz für das Auto. 24-Stunden-Pförtnerdienst mit Postservice. Und wenn sie im Urlaub ist, gießt jemand ihre Blumen.

Belle genießt den Komfort, fühlt sich in der Anlage sicher. Sie versteht die Kritik an diesen Wohnanlagen nicht – für sie macht es keinen Unterschied, ob ein Hausbesitzer einen Zaun um sein Grundstück zieht oder ob Wohnsiedlungen gemeinschaftlich für ihren Schutz sorgen. Und auch das Argument, man schotte sich sozial ab, lässt sie nicht gelten: Was uns da immer nachgesagt wird, hier geschlossene Gesellschaft, und die schotten sich ab, das ist nicht so. Wir haben auch viele Bekannte außerhalb, die auch uns besuchen kommen. Und wir unternehmen auch viel in Potsdam. Es ist nicht so, dass wir uns ausschließen und sagen, wir sind hier ganz für uns.

Stadtforscher, Politikwissenschaftler und Soziologen in Deutschland diskutieren über das Entstehen von Gated Communities jedoch kritisch. Volker Eichener, Politikwissenschaftler an der Universität Düsseldorf, beschäftigt sich seit einigen Jahren mit dem Phänomen und hält es für einen Trugschluss wohlhabender Bevölkerungsgruppen, dass sie sich durch das Wohnen in solch einer Siedlung absichern könnten. Vielmehr wäre das Gegenteil der Fall:

Nämlich dadurch machen sie sich sichtbar. Sie rufen Neid hervor. Und sie laden auch gerade dazu ein, Opfer zu werden von allen möglichen Formen von Konflikten, Anfeindungen, und dann auch echter Kriminalität.

Richtige Gated Communities mit Sicherheitszaun und Pförtner bilden in Deutschland aber ohnehin eine Ausnahme. Vielmehr gibt es hier einen neuen Trend – eine milde Ausprägung der städtebaulichen Abgrenzung von Siedlungen.

Siedlungen müssen nicht unbedingt über meterhohe Zäune und Überwachungskameras verfügen, um sich von der Umgebung abzugrenzen. Volker Eichner untersucht vielmehr auch die „milderen“ Formen von Abschottung wohlhabender Bevölkerungsgruppen in Neubausiedlungen: Es gibt aber auch milde Formen, die noch nicht mal Tore vorsehen, die aber sozusagen optische Grenzen definieren, sodass sich Menschen, die dort nicht wohnen, in die Siedlung eigentlich nicht hinein trauen. Das kann man durch eine geschickte optische Gestaltung so erreichen. Teilweise ist dann auch der Bodenbelag, die Pflasterung anders, sodass man das Gefühl hat, ich bin hier fremd, ich bin hier nicht willkommen.

Siedlungen können sich auch durch bauliche Maßnahmen – ein anderer Straßenbelag, eine Hecke, eine Schranke – von ihrer Nachbarschaft abgrenzen. Sie vermitteln dem Besucher damit, dass er an dieser Stelle fremd ist. Er weiß vielleicht nicht, ob er das Gelände überhaupt so einfach betreten darf.

Aber ist das verwerflich, sich von seiner Umgebung abzugrenzen? Sicherheit zu suchen? Gerade vor dem Hintergrund der vielen Krisen weltweit und dem Auseinanderklaffen armer und reicher Schichten in Deutschland? Diese Debatte gilt es weiter zu führen. Der Politikwissenschaftler Volker Eichener hofft jedoch, dass der Trend hin zur architektonischen Abschottung nicht weiter um sich greift. Er findet, man sollte sich bemühen, die Separierung der Bevölkerungsgruppen nicht noch weiter voranzutreiben. Sondern im Gegenteil Möglichkeiten der Begegnung schaffen. *(557 words)*

Task

Imagine that you are taking part in an international conference on gated communities. Summarise views in Germany on the topic on the basis of the radio broadcast transcript. *(30)*

Lösungsvorschläge

Textaufgabe

1. ***Hinweis:*** *How to approach the task:*
Step 1: Read the text carefully and highlight the information given on Kleinfontein.
Step 2: Start off with an umbrella sentence containing the author, the source and the topic.
Step 3: Omit minor details and limit yourself to a maximum of 200 words.

The text at hand, an extract from an article by Sudarsan Raghavan published in *The Guardian*, deals with a gated community called Kleinfontein in South Africa. Kleinfontein is an all-white Afrikaner settlement that excludes black people, Jews and Catholics as well as English speakers. To live there, you need to meet three criteria: You must speak Afrikaans, you have to be a Protestant Christian and your ancestry must date back to the Dutch settlers who left the British Cape Colony and settled in the interior of South Africa in the early 19th century.
The inhabitants of this gated community view their settlement as an Afrikaner enclave where they can protect themselves against affirmative action and high crime rates for which they blame the black South Africans. Furthermore, they claim that they can maintain their cultural heritage and speak their own language.
Local black leaders view Kleinfontein as a remnant of the racist Apartheid system and demand that it be closed down. *(161 words)*

2. ***Hinweis:*** *How to approach the task:*
Step 1: Consider that Apartheid came to an end in the early 1990s, yet communities like Kleinfontein are still based on exclusion.
Step 2: Look at the cartoon closely and consider the visual elements before you determine the message.
Step 3: Examine the image of South Africa that is conveyed in both the article and the cartoon.

From both the article and the cartoon we obtain the impression that South Africa is a deeply fragmented nation still dealing with the repercussions of the Apartheid regime. This stands in contrast to South Africa's image as the so-called Rainbow Nation, in which people now live together peacefully and enjoy equal rights regardless of their race, religion, or social and cultural background.
The article about Kleinfontein makes it clear that long after Apartheid came to an end there are still racial barriers that separate whites and Afrikaners, in particular from the rest of the population. There are white South Africans who exclude others from their heavily guarded settlements while at the same time claiming that they are not racists. What they fear is crime, which they blame black South Africans for, and they also want to protect themselves against affirmative action programmes which are intended to promote racial equality with the help of quota regulations. Some

Afrikaners also feel unwelcome in post-Apartheid South Africa and therefore isolate themselves from the rest of society to cultivate their heritage.
Of course, the black majority resents these settlements, which are painful reminders of former oppressive Apartheid laws and racial segregation. The exclusion of black South Africans from these settlements probably also runs along economic lines, as most blacks would not be able to afford homes in exclusive places like Kleinfontein, even if they were allowed to buy them. It is therefore understandable that all-white communities are a provocation to the black population.
The text shows that long after the abolishment of Apartheid the racial divide has yet to be overcome, and the cartoon points in a similar direction. It presents the late former president Nelson Mandela as an old man who needs his walking stick to stand upright. His facial expression indicates that he is agonised and troubled. On his hand is sitting a white dove with the word "Peace" written on it. The dove is losing a feather, which is about to fall on top of a dead dove on the ground. This dove has the word "Justice" written on it. The image that is presented of South Africa in this cartoon is that despite the abolition of Apartheid, peace is fragile, and justice seems to be dead. The basic problem addressed here could be the lack of social and economic justice in modern South Africa, with blacks still being at a disadvantage when it comes to education and employment. As a result, many get caught in a vicious circle of poverty and crime. This has led to a steep rise in crime rates, which motivates white people to move to gated communities – a development that does not contribute to an integrated and just society. All in all, the message of the cartoon could be that the reconciliation process is endangered by social, racial and economic inequities in everyday life. So both the text and the cartoon show that justice and equality have not yet been achieved. *(495 words)*

3. ***Hinweis:*** *How to approach the task:*
Step 1: Devise a chart in which you collect arguments for and against permitting gated communities like Kleinfontein.
Step 2: Weigh up the arguments, come to a conclusion and take a stand.

It is a pity that so many Afrikaners only feel at home in whites-only enclaves with armed guards and surveillance cameras. In principle, I am convinced that they have the right to cultivate their heritage and speak their language. In addition, I believe that individuals have the right to choose where they want to live and with whom. Nevertheless, are the rights of a few individuals more important than social coherence in South Africa?
Whites-only settlements that are based on the exclusion of others along the lines of race, religion or income are a provocation to the black majority in South Africa, and other parts of the population. The idea of exclusion stands in contrast to the democratic principle of equality and runs counter to the idea of a pluralistic nation where people of all colours live together peacefully. Furthermore, these villages are remnants of the former oppressive apartheid system that painfully remind blacks of decades of suppression and racial segregation. As such, those settlements jeopardise

social harmony, and they pose a threat to the process of integration and reconciliation. These settlements also spark protest because they stand for the concept of "white superiority".
I wish that the government and the people in South Africa could find a solution to the huge social and economic divide in South African society because security and social peace are guaranteed first and foremost by economic prosperity and democratic participation. If the social and economic divide were overcome, there would be less crime, and probably less demand for houses in exclusionary villages. Yet, at present these obstacles have not yet been overcome, and all-white settlements stand in the way of integration. That is why I feel with the black population and strongly favour the prohibition of settlements that are based on undemocratic, exclusionary principles. *(300 words)*

Sprachmittlung

Hinweis: *How to approach the task:*
Step 1: Read the text carefully and concentrate on the different attitudes to gated communities.
Step 2: Start off with an umbrella sentence containing the source and the topic.
Step 3: Write a maximum of 250 words.

From a radio feature on gated communities we find out that there is an increasing demand for expensive apartments in gated communities in Germany. These communities, which look like holiday resorts, offer comfortable services like 24-hour reception, high fences and surveillance cameras as well as underground car parks. Inhabitants, however, claim that they are not isolating themselves from the rest of society, as they do have visitors from outside, for example.
Yet, social scientists view this trend critically. They point out that affluent people falsely believe that gated communities provide security. On the contrary, the inhabitants become more visible, and that causes envy. As a result, they are more likely to fall victim to crime.
Currently, Germany is witnessing a new trend towards separate communities of a milder kind that work without cameras and gates. There are optical barriers, such as specially designed pavements, hedges or barriers, which give passers-by the feeling that they are not welcome, and make them doubt whether they have the right to walk there. Intellectuals and scientists are critical of these developments, which they attribute to global crises and the increasing divide between rich and poor in Germany. They emphasise that they would prefer more places for people to meet than secluded areas.
(208 words)

Klausur 4: London

Hörverstehen 30 min.

Track 1

Is London what it used to be?

Study the tasks below carefully before listening. Listen to the podcast twice. Do not tick more than the number of correct answers set in a task. *(20)*

1. Name the two reasons the journalist suggests for the increase in domestic tourism. *(2)*

   a) ____

   b) ____

2. Tick the two correct answers. *(2)*

   The specialist subjects of Caroline Dunmore and John Finn are …

   - ☐ history of art and architecture.
   - ☐ hygiene and sanitation.
   - ☐ the natural sciences.
   - ☐ politics and social studies.
   - ☐ printing and publishing.

3. Complete the text. *(5)*

   In order to become a guide, people can participate in a course at the University of Westminster, which lasts ____________________, and finally take two practical tests, one in ____________________ and one ____________________. Furthermore, they have to do two written pieces, one under ____________________ and the other as a piece of ____________________.

4. Name the three imperial units still used today which were introduced by the Weights and Measurements Act of the 1820s. *(3)*

   a) ____

   b) ____

   c) ____

5. Complete the table. *(2)*

The London demonstration in 1887:

	people	guards
number		

6. Complete the text. *(4)*

In the 1880s Britain was going through ____________________,

and there was no ____________________ to help the poor and unemployed. To protest against that situation, there was a demonstration during which a number of people died, which is why that day was also known as ____________________, a name that has now been forgotten due to ____________________.

7. Tick the <u>two</u> correct answers. *(2)*

The London tourist attractions mentioned in the audio text are …

- ☐ Big Ben.
- ☐ Nelson's Column.
- ☐ Trafalgar Square.
- ☐ St. Paul's Cathedral.
- ☐ Tower Bridge.

Textaufgabe 90 min.

The streets are ours: A London walking tour through the eyes of the homeless

Mike doesn't have a minibus, and he's in north London rather than California, but he does a good impression of one of those Hollywood homes tour guides all the same.

[…] Then when Mike departs from the Hollywood model and turns me around to look at the church behind us, things become rather more compelling. This, he explains, is the food bank where, not long ago, he was forced by circumstances to come himself.

[…] It's all part of the experience of an Unseen Tour, a walk around London with someone who knows it from a rather different point of view to your typical guide, because they once lived on the streets.

Unseen Tours has been running for nearly five years, having started in 2010 when a volunteer network called the Sock Mob – which handed out socks (as well as other clothes and food) to homeless people – concluded that there were other, more powerful ways of helping people than simply handing things out.

Some of the guides came through those meetings, others from contacts with local charities; all of them have spent some time living on the street, although they don't get kicked off the roster the moment they are in a more stable situation.

Guides get 60 % of the income and the rest goes towards the not-for-profit organisers' running costs. Unseen Tours is at pains to make clear that this is not poverty tourism: the idea is not to peer at the homeless, but to infuse a conventional tour with deeper authority.

When we meet at Chalk Farm tube station, another guy approaches, asking for money, and the difference between his bearing and Mike's could hardly be more pointed. Mike – wiry and white-haired, and smartly dressed in red trousers, short coat and flat cap – is at pains to point out that the situation he found himself in wasn't the result of drug or alcohol abuse. His essential sortedness is a large part of why he's such a charming and confident guide.

But it's also shamefully clear that a guide designation makes those of us who might otherwise look right past a homeless person pay rapt attention. London's streets, you realise, are probably full of equally good guides: it's just that no one has ever thought to ask them. Mike has a long history in Camden, having started to hang out at the Roundhouse in the 70s. He lived in the area for years – long before the series of mishaps that left him on the streets […].

[…] "I used to work in the City as a facilities manager," he says. "Then the banking crisis struck and things went downhill fast."

After losing his job, he moved abroad, hoping to ride out the recession as an English teacher. But when he came back he still couldn't find work. After months of sofa-surfing, he wound up homeless.

[…] Mike's story, I'm happy to report, doesn't finish there. Things got decidedly better, and Unseen Tours played a big part in the upturn. But I won't ruin his punchline. If you want to hear the ending […] you'll just have to book for yourself. *(540 words)*

Tasks

1. Sum up Mike's story. *(10)*
2. Explain the history of *Unseen Tours* as well as the idea behind it. *(20)*
3. "Unseen Tours is at pains to make clear that this is not poverty tourism: the idea is not to peer at the homeless, but to infuse a conventional tour with deeper authority." (ll. 17–19)
   Comment on this quote. Write up to 250 words. *(30)*

Lösungsvorschläge

Hörverstehen

Transkript: Is London what it used to be?

[…] Tourism is big business, generating £ 115 billion a year for the UK economy, and whether as a result of the age of austerity encouraging people to holiday at home, or even a re-engagement with our heritage, domestic tourism is making an ever greater contribution to this overall figure.

This is all good news for London's walking guides, who primarily develop walks for interested locals, or those keen to get under the skin of the city. So I donned my walking shoes and headed off to meet some of the people who are setting the standard and raising the bar in the rather crowded world of guiding.

Dr Caroline Dunmore: My specialist subjects are history of art and architecture, and history of science.

John Finn: I'm particularly interested in printing and publishing, the way people lived, housing, things like that.

Caroline Dunmore and her colleague John Finn are both qualified walking guides and head up the diploma of special study in tour guiding at the University of Westminster.

Alex Bingham: I've been talking to people about this in the process of making this podcast and the amount of people who are surprised that there is a course that allows you to become a guide, I think people just think you have an idea and then you head out onto the streets and you start telling people about it.

[…]

John Finn: It's a year long course and through that time the students have to attend a weekly session at the University of Westminster, appear every other Saturday on the street to train themselves as guides on the streets …

Dr Caroline Dunmore: Be trained by us.

John Finn: And be trained by us, exactly. And they have to take two practical examinations: one in the London Transport Museum, one out on the streets. This summer it was in Regent's Park and environs, and they have to write two written pieces. One under exam conditions, and the other is a piece of submitted research.

Alex Bingham: So it's not for the faint-hearted?

John Finn: No.

[…]

Alex Bingham: Amidst the hustle and bustle of Trafalgar Square, one of London's central tourist spots, Caroline, you've brought me to the very edge of the square to something which I've certainly never taken any notice of before. It's a big, brass plaque with various knobs and bits and bobs sticking out of it. What is it?

Dr Caroline Dunmore: Well, this is something that was embedded here to give the weight and measures the imperial units. So back in the 1820s, there was a weights and measures act which introduced the imperial units that we all learned when we were at school. The inch, the foot, the yard and so on. And later on, in the 1870s, they embedded this plaque here, which actually defines, it gives the definitions of those measures. And we can walk along this north edge of Trafalgar Square and we'll see markings for other units like the very old-fashioned ones like the pole and the perch and the link and the chain that none of us can ever remember how to define. This is something that guides love. Trafalgar Square is one of the most famous spots in the world, but even born and bred Londoners probably don't know that there's this unusual feature here.

Alex Bingham: John, did you know about this?

John Finn: I did actually, but Caroline's quite right that it's one of those unknown bits of London. The other unknown thing of course is that we're standing in a very iconic space in London where tourists come to look at Nelson's Column and enjoy the sun as we are today, but they may not be aware that actually there's another history to this space as well. Back in the 1880s Britain was undergoing yet another of its cycle of economic recessions. And during that time, there was no welfare state to support those who are unemployed, and there was a great deal of agitation about those people who were out of work and poor and their families starving, so they organised a demonstration to come down from Clerkenwell in north of London down through the streets into this square to protest about the situation. That was in November 1887, and huge numbers of people assembled in the square and they were addressed by people like William Morris, I'm not sure how in the days before microphones and loudspeakers how people heard him, but this square was packed with over 150,000 people. However, also the government had ordered out 600 lifeguards and grenadier guards, who attacked the crowd and several people died or were crushed to death. It was called Bloody Sunday, a name that's probably been forgotten because of the Irish Troubles, but it was named "Bloody Sunday" at that time. It became a big sort of cause célèbre of liberals and radicals of the day.

Alex Bingham: I must admit, standing here surrounded by tourists, people enjoying the sun and looking at the fountains, I had absolutely no idea that something so chilling and tragic actually took place here. That seems the wonderful thing about the walks that you do, it's just opening people's eyes to a city that they never even really knew existed.

Dr Caroline Dunmore: I think that's absolutely right, Alex. What we're doing is peeling back the layers and telling different stories, and I think the other thing that John and I have been wanting to show today is the way that there are very different stories that you can tell. So I've been telling you some things about the history of science in London, John's been talking about social history, history of protest, and so on. And there are all sorts of other different angles that you can take as you know, so it's fascinating, just so many different stories that you can dig out from what we see around us in London.

[…] *(985 words)*

Hinweis: This podcast is an interview, so there are different people involved. Be prepared for the varying speed and pronunciation of the different speakers.
Concerning the multiple-choice tasks, make sure you only tick the number of correct answers indicated.
The wording of the tasks may be different from the audio, i. e. sentences may have been reworded or synonyms may be used.
Concerning the tasks to be answered in your own words, the solutions given are suggestions. You do not always need to use the original wording, but your answer must nevertheless contain the aspects mentioned.

1. a) a result of (the age of) austerity
   b) re-engagement with our/one's heritage

2. The specialist subjects of Caroline Dunmore and John Finn are …
   - [x] history of art and architecture.
   - [ ] hygiene and sanitation.
   - [ ] the natural sciences.
   - [ ] politics and social studies.
   - [x] printing and publishing.

3. In order to become a guide, people can participate in a course at the University of Westminster, which lasts **a/one year**, and finally take two practical tests, one in **the London Transport Museum** and one **out on the street(s)**. Furthermore, they have to do two written pieces, one under **exam conditions** and the other as a piece of **(submitted) research**.

4. a) inch
   b) foot
   c) yard

5. The London demonstration in 1887:

	people	guards
number	(over) 150,000	600

6. In the 1880s Britain was going through **(a cycle of) economic recessions**, and there was no **welfare (state)** to help the poor and unemployed. To protest against that situation, there was a demonstration during which a number of people died, which is why that day was also known as **Bloody Sunday**, a name that has now been forgotten due to **the Irish Troubles**.

7. The London tourist attractions mentioned in the audio text are …
   - [ ] Big Ben.
   - [x] Nelson's Column.
   - [x] Trafalgar Square.
   - [ ] St. Paul's Cathedral.
   - [ ] Tower Bridge.

Textaufgabe

1. ***Hinweis:*** *In this type of task ("Sum up …), you are required to give a brief summary of the basic ideas in a text in your own words, in this case of the information given about Mike. Read the text attentively to find the relevant information. Start your answer with a sentence that introduces the topic (topic sentence). Use a neutral style without any personal comments and bear in mind the length of your text as indicated by the number of credits.*

   In order to sum up Mike's story as presented in the article, it is first necessary to mention that he currently works with Unseen Tours, a London-based programme that offers walking tours with people who are or have been homeless.
   Mike used to be employed as a facilities manager in the centre of London, but the impact of an economic crisis cost him his job. As a consequence, he left the country temporarily in the hope of surviving his economic situation by working as an English teacher. On returning, Mike was still not able to find employment or accommodation so he had to stay at other people's houses before he ended up living on the streets and eventually going to a food bank. However, since working with Unseen Tours, Mike's situation has improved considerably. *(134 words)*

2. ***Hinweis:*** *Here you are asked to explain the background of an idea in your own words, in this case Unseen Tours and its history. Read the whole text carefully in order to find the relevant information. Remember to divide the task into two parts: first elaborate on the history of Unseen Tours, then define the idea behind it. Use a neutral style without any personal comments and bear in mind the length of your text as indicated by the number of credits.*

   The history of Unseen Tours began in 2010 with a network of volunteers giving homeless people food and clothes, such as socks, which earned the network the name "Sock Mob". However, they eventually came to the conclusion that instead of just handing things out, they could help people in ways that were more powerful. Nowadays, Unseen Tours is a non-profit organisation that offers walking tours through London guided by homeless people.
   The foremost idea behind Unseen Tours is a charitable one. People who have been living on the streets for some time get the chance to improve and stabilise their

situation. The money earned from the tours benefits everybody involved, as 60 % of it goes to the homeless guides and the remaining 40 % pays for the running costs. Secondly, another idea is to make it possible for tourists to see London from a different perspective. Having spent at least some time on the streets, the guides of Unseen Tours fill the otherwise customary walks with a more profound meaning. The organisers of the tours explicitly stress the fact that the tours are not "poverty tourism". *(187 words)*

3. ***Hinweis:*** *Here you are asked for your opinion on a quote from the text. A comment should be composed of three different parts: introduction, main part and conclusion.*
In an introduction, you could refer to current events, quote famous people or statistics or mention personal experience, for example. Bear in mind that you should state a theme at the end of the introduction.
In the main part of a comment, you can present the positive and negative aspects of a topic in different paragraphs. Remember to present your idea at the beginning of each paragraph.
In the conclusion, you should not include any new arguments or examples but state your personal opinion explicitly in one final paragraph.

The example of Mike's story as presented in the text shows what you can achieve by giving homeless people the opportunity to make use of their special knowledge: Mike, for example, has improved his personal situation with his walking tours through London. However, the idea of having homeless people as guides for walking tours could be a controversial issue.

On the one hand, some people might think that Unseen Tours is taking advantage of the sensationalist aspect. Some tourists are attracted by the opportunity of peering at "real" homeless people. As a consequence, the guides might feel exploited or humiliated if other people are fascinated by or make money out of their homelessness.

While it is true that sensationalism violates the dignity of the homeless, Unseen Tours attach great importance to the fact that they are helping homeless people to help themselves and regain control of their lives. Instead of drawing welfare benefits, the homeless can earn their living by working as tour guides. As the organisers of the not-for-profit tours only need to cover their expenses, the guides receive 60 % of the income.

In my opinion, the charitable idea behind Unseen Tours outweighs the sensationalist aspect. To conclude, I think that the tours with homeless or formerly homeless guides are a model from which everybody can benefit. *(217 words)*

Klausur 5: Modern Life

Hörverstehen 45 min.

Track 2

Digital breadcrumbs: the data trail we leave behind us

Study the tasks below carefully before listening. Listen to the podcast twice. Do not tick more than the number of correct answers set in a task. *(20)*

1. Complete the following sentences. *(3)*

   a) When Amanda woke up …
   - ☐ she listened to the BBC weather report.
   - ☐ she checked her phone for messages.
   - ☐ she checked the weather on her BBC app.

   b) Amanda sent a message via Facebook telling a friend …
   - ☐ she was about to leave the house.
   - ☐ she would be arriving at the university in a moment.
   - ☐ she would be late today.

   c) Amanda's friend could tell that she …
   - ☐ hadn't left the house.
   - ☐ was already halfway to SOAS[1].
   - ☐ was still on the Underground.

2. Name two electronic cards which give away information about your daily movements. *(2)*

   a) ______________________________

   b) ______________________________

3. Complete the text with words from the podcast. *(5)*

   When you use a smartphone or a computer you leave a ______________ behind you. There is constant background ______________ between the phone, the cell towers and the ______________. So there are all these apps that are getting ______________ about your phone, and about your ______________.

[1]SOAS: School of Oriental and African Studies, University of London

4. Tick the <u>two</u> correct answers. *(2)*

When you do a search on Google …

☐ the data is stored on your phone.

☐ your data will be stored on Google servers.

☐ you can decide where your data is stored.

☐ you do not know where in the world your data is stored.

☐ your data will not be stored.

5. Decide whether these statements are true or false. *(8)*

	true	false
a) As a user there is a way to find out what data is stored about you.	☐	☐
b) Facebook and Google Maps, for example, were mentioned by many people as a way to leave a digital trail.	☐	☐
c) Most people were pretty much aware of the data trails they leave behind.	☐	☐
d) In contrast to WhatsApp, the Asian messenger app Hike does not ask for personal information.	☐	☐
e) Collecting masses of data is synonymous to earning good money.	☐	☐
f) For big companies, data is the new currency.	☐	☐
g) It seems as if giving away our data is the price for using a service for free.	☐	☐
h) In our digital world, we cannot avoid leaving digital traces.	☐	☐

Textaufgabe 60 min.

Dan Pearce: from dreaming of video game design to doing it for real

When Dan Pearce was in primary school, he told his friends that he had won a competition to have one of his ideas made into a video game by an international video game publisher. It was a lie, but one Pearce coolly upheld, inviting his friends to pitch in ideas for how the game could be improved. “It basically turned into a two-year exercise in designing as a group and getting feedback on my ideas,” he recalls today. “That said, I do still feel very guilty about maintaining the lie for so long.”

Thanks to this formative experience, by the age of 10, Pearce, who lives in Maidenhead, Berkshire, knew that he wanted to become a game designer. The following year he bought a copy of RPG Maker, a simple game-making tool for Sony’s PlayStation. The first game he made was a pastiche of his favourite Nintendo games – The Legend of Zelda, Final Fantasy and Pokémon. "It was basically just me taking aesthetic elements that I liked in various pieces of media," he says. "There was an island floating in the sky because I liked a Gorillaz music video. I once bunked off school for two weeks so that I could just work on that game."

Despite his investment, Pearce eventually scrapped the project and began learning how to program games in earnest. Ten Second Ninja was the first fruit of his study, a platform game in which each level requires you to defeat all of the on-screen enemies within 10 seconds. The diminutive ninja you control has just two attacks, one of which, a hurled shuriken, can be used only three times per level, forcing players to make snapshot, yet crucial, decisions. "One half of my brain is obsessed with systems and pure, gameplay-focused design," he says. "This is the kind of design that I end up doing the most, and find the easiest: spatial games that are essentially just maths problems in disguise."

In 2013, Pearce released a different kind of game, one that he says comes from a different part of his design sensibility. Castles in the Sky is a simple, wistful game (Pearce describes it as an "interactive storybook"), in which you play a young boy who leaves the Earth by leaping between clouds. The game lasts only a few minutes and is sound-tracked by a melancholic piano score, written and performed by Pearce's collaborator, Jack de Quidt. It is, to Pearce's mind, a rumination on growing up.

"I find this kind of work a lot more emotionally exhausting," says Pearce. "It requires a lot of self-assessment and contemplation. The game was a way of trying to evoke the awe and energy of being a kid. In a way, it helped me let go of childhood. It's made me much happier and a lot more comfortable about turning into an adult."

(476 words)

Tasks

1. Outline Dan Pearce's career as a video game designer. *(10)*
2. Analyse Dan Pearce's fascination with video game programming. *(15)*
3. Write a blog entry on the (continued) controversy about video games. *(25)*

Lösungsvorschläge

Hörverstehen

Transkript: Digital breadcrumbs: the data trail we leave behind us

Once upon a time, in the land of Great Britain, Amanda woke up to the sun shining on a bright Monday morning. Before she got out of bed, she opened the BBC weather app to check the weather for the day ahead on her phone. […] She quickly took a shower, made some breakfast, brushed her teeth and left the house. Amanda used Facebook to send a message to her friend telling him she was almost at SOAS. Her friend replied: "No you're not! Your message location says you're still at home!" Oops. Amanda was busted! She tapped her Oyster Card at the Underground Station and read the news on The Guardian app using the Wifi available underground. Arriving at Russell Square Station, she bought coffee at a café using her contactless card and made her way to SOAS for her first lecture of the day. Amanda was blissfully unaware that her morning schedule had created a trail of "digital breadcrumbs". This means that she can be traced and tracked through the apps she accessed and the technology she used. But what does that really mean? Who has access to this information? And can it be used against us? Are we all blissfully unaware like Amanda? And should we be worried?

Narrator: Welcome to "Digital Breadcrumbs" […]. Our podcast explores the digital trails or digital footprints we create in our daily lives. The majority of applications we use require our location information. We willingly tag ourselves in specific locations through social media platforms, and freely use contactless cards and debit cards, which give both retailers, banks and various other organisations information about our daily movements. We are constantly monitored on CCTV and everything we research online is data being collected or stored. In this episode, we'll be talking to lecturers and students to discover the real cost of our digital footsteps. So first of all, what exactly is a digital trail?

Dr. Elisa Oreglia: A "digital trail" is a trace that you leave behind you. It's almost like breadcrumbs. Sometimes intentionally, sometimes unintentionally when you use a mobile phone, but also when you use a computer, when you use really any kind of technology that has a chip in it.

N.: We interviewed Elisa Oreglia, a lecturer in Global Digital Cultures at SOAS, to find out more about our digital footprints.

E.O.: Basically, when you have a phone, you have a series of censors and you have this constant background communication between the phone and the cell towers, but also if it's connected online between the phone and the internet so there are all these apps that are getting information about your phone, about your environment.

N.: Dr. Oreglia tells us that all this communication is sent elsewhere, it doesn't just stay on your phone. And it's constant. It accumulates over time. But where is it being stored? According to Dr. Oreglia, it is going to several different places. The signal on your mobile phone tells your mobile phone network where you are. […] We then proceeded to ask Dr. Oreglia about what happens to data we have researched.

E.O.: When you do a search on Google, that information goes through Google Servers. So first of all it has to travel through a variety of internet service providers and then it gets stored into Google Servers. And they can really be anywhere in the world. Google has several data centres scattered around the world. So, you're not really sure of where they will be. It's not like, if you are doing a search in the UK, the data will necessarily be kept in Google Servers in the UK.

N.: Dr. Oreglia then spoke about legislation processes and laws that may protect individuals from digital privacy breaching in the UK.

E.O.: [...] So, there is the UK government website about the Data Protection Act, that has some very useful information just for regular users. It lays out in a very clear manner the way that you can ask an organisation or a company for what kind of information they have about you. And these companies and organisations are actually required to answer you.

N.: As a part of our research we wanted to find out if any of the students or others at SOAS had any idea about what data they are sharing and where it might be going. So we asked them, and we got some interesting results. [...] We spoke to some individuals who had a good grasp of what digital trails are and whether or not they were creating them. Some were less sure about it, while some admitted to having never thought about it. [...] The findings from our interviews made us realise that a lot of people mentioned Facebook or Google Maps as a form of digital trail they were creating. But most, like Amanda, were pretty unaware of the extent of their digital trails extending to their daily use of contactless cards and the majority of applications on their phones. [...] We also spoke with Murali Shanmugavelan, who convenes the MA Media in Development course at SOAS. He told us about a rival to the instant messenger application WhatsApp that is particularly popular in South Asia, called Hike. He shared his personal experience that upon downloading the app he was required to give permission for all manner of personal information. It makes one think, "What kind of information do apps like this need?" And what kind of access do they require?

Murali Shanmugavelan: Practically everything. And there you have to have some sense of ethics. Why do you need to access my multimedia files to launch a chat app?

N.: A question that I'm sure many of us have asked. He tells us about a perception related to the scale of economy attached to data.

M.S.: Data is a big business. Big data is big business. But it's a red herring. WhatsApp is the most influential chat app right now, but it hasn't made any money. So, if you're talking about killer app, bigger data = tons of money, that's not the case. But somehow, we actually have bought into this idea that digital data equals money.

N.: [...] The data we produce as individuals mostly benefits big corporations because as Dr. Oreglia has mentioned, this data, when segregated, becomes a highly valuable form of currency. Should we then as producers of data benefit from the money that we help generate or is the fact that we use these services for free sufficient enough to serve as a form of payment in return for our data? Just like Amanda, our lives continue in the digital world and leave digital breadcrumbs along the way. Armed with new information on this matter, we stand at the crossroads; will this trail of data we leave benefit or harm us in the long run? But life goes on in a bustling city [like] London. Amanda once again woke up to the sound of the alarm, checked the BBC Weather app and continued to provide valuable information without taking any interest in it. […] *(1 183 words)*

Hinweis:

1. a) (ll. 2/3): "… she opened the BBC weather app … on her phone …"
b) (l. 5): "… a message to her friend telling him she was almost at SOAS."
c) (l. 6): " 'No you're not! Your message location says you're still at home!' "

2. (ll. 17–20): "We … freely use contactless cards and debit cards, which give both retailers, banks and various other organisations information about our daily movements."

3. ll. 24–33

4. (ll. 39–41): "… information goes through Google Servers. First of all it has to travel through a variety of internet service providers and then it gets stored into Google Servers … anywhere in the world."

5. a) (ll. 47–50): "… Data Protection Act … lays out … the way that you can ask an organisation or a company for what kind of information they have about you."
b) (ll. 57–59): "… a lot of people mentioned Facebook or Google Maps as a form of digital trail they were creating."
c) (ll. 59/60): "… most … were pretty unaware of the extent of their digital trails …"
d) (ll. 63–65): "… instant messenger application … that is particularly popular in South Asia, called Hike … upon downloading the app he was required to give permission for all manner of personal information."
e) (ll. 72–74): "WhatsApp is the most influential chat app right now, but it hasn't made any money. So, if you're talking about killer app + bigger data = tons of money, that's not the case."
f) (ll. 76–78): "The data we produce … mostly benefit big corporations because … this data, when segregated, becomes a highly valuable form of currency."
g) (ll. 79/80): "… is the fact that we use these services for free sufficient enough to serve as a form of payment in return for our data?"
h) (ll. 80–82): "… our lives continue in the digital world and leave digital breadcrumbs along the way."

1. a) When Amanda woke up …

   ☐ she listened to the BBC weather report.
   ☐ she checked her phone for messages.
   ☑ she checked the weather on her BBC app.

   b) Amanda sent a message via Facebook telling a friend …

   ☐ she was about to leave the house.
   ☑ she would be arriving at the university in a moment.
   ☐ she would be late today.

c) Amanda's friend could tell that she ...
   - [x] hadn't left the house.
   - [ ] was already halfway to SOAS.
   - [ ] was still on the Underground.

2. a) contactless cards
   b) debit cards

3. When you use a smartphone or a computer you leave a **(digital) trail/ trace** behind you. There is constant background **communication** between the phone, the cell towers and the **internet**. So there are all these apps that are getting **information** about your phone, and about your **environment**.

4. When you do a search on Google ...
   - [ ] the data is stored on your phone.
   - [x] your data will be stored on Google servers.
   - [ ] you can decide where your data is stored.
   - [x] you do not know where in the world your data is stored.
   - [ ] your data will not be stored.

5. Decide whether these statements are true or false.

	true	false
a) As a user there is a way to find out what data is stored about you.	✓	
b) Facebook and Google Maps, for example, were mentioned by many people as a way to leave a digital trail.	✓	
c) Most people were pretty much aware of the data trails they leave behind.		✓
d) In contrast to WhatsApp, the Asian messenger app Hike does not ask for personal information.		✓
e) Collecting masses of data is synonymous to earning good money.		✓
f) For big companies, data is the new currency.	✓	
g) It seems as if giving away our data is the price for using a service for free.	✓	
h) In our digital world, we cannot avoid leaving digital traces.	✓	

Textaufgabe

1. ***Hinweis:*** *The article informs you about Dan Pearce, a professional video game programmer. You are asked to retrace his career and list the steps which led him to what he is now. Read the whole article carefully, marking the years given and Dan's respective ages which will help you establish a chronological order of his development. The most relevant turning points in Dan's career include:*
   - *he first became interested in computer games when he was still in primary school*
   - *at age 11 he bought the software which enabled him to design games himself*
   - *as he was not satisfied with his first attempts, he began to study video game design from scratch*
   - *in 2013, he designed a role-playing game which included personal experiences.*

   Today, Dan is a recognised and successful video game programmer. He first became interested in creating video games when he was still in primary school. He successfully talked his friends into helping him develop ideas for a new game. When he was 10, he was convinced that he wanted to take up game designing as his profession. At 11, he began to make his dream come true by purchasing a software which enabled him to program video games. The first result of his efforts was a game which he pieced together from elements of some of his favourite computer games at that time. Although he had spent a lot of time and money on developing the game, Dan was not satisfied and began to study video game design from scratch. With the creation of this first original game Dan discovered what he could do and liked best, i. e. designing games which basically represent mathematical problems. In 2013, he published a game which included some of his own personal experiences as a young boy. *(174 words)*

2. ***Hinweis:*** *Here, you are required to dig more deeply and find possible explanations for Dan Pearce's fascination with video game programming. The article does not mention his motivations directly. However, when looking closely at Dan's development, it can be inferred why his enthusiasm as a boy eventually made him take up video programming as his profession. It is likely that the reason why he was so strongly attracted to the activity was because he could be creative and found pleasure in working out puzzles for others. The fact that designing and selling the games also brings financial rewards is not mentioned in the text, and might therefore be considered as a secondary motive for Dan's enduring fascination.*

   Although Dan's motivation to become a video game programmer or designer is not expressly stated in the text, it seems obvious that this occupation has long exerted a fascination for him which has never left him. Even when he was in primary school, Dan claimed his ideas of a video game were going to be made into a real game by an international company. He was so dedicated to game designing that he used this lie to get his friends to contribute ideas to the design of the game.

While creating his first game, Dan was so fascinated and involved that he did not have time for anything else and even played truant for two weeks. Dan's latest game was somehow different from what he had designed up to then, in as much as he profited from the game himself. It helped him to come to terms with the transition from childhood to adolescence.
Although Dan Pearce is a professional video game programmer, the financial aspects of the business are not mentioned, which could mean that money is not one of his major incentives. Instead, creativity and inventiveness seem to be the main driving forces behind Dan's occupation. *(198 words)*

3. ***Hinweis:*** *First, try to find a concise or catchy headline for your blog entry. After that, start your text with an introduction, for example: digital games are popular but they have always raised controversy. Then go on with the main part:*
a) criticism:
   - *gamers neglect their social lives*
   - *loss of communication skills*
   - *video games: promoting violent and aggressive behaviour, lack of empathy*

b) defence:
   - *games with violent content for adults only*
   - *today players are rewarded for patience and skill rather than violence*
   - *benefits for gamers: better academic achievements; spatial ability*

conclusion:
- *unfair generalisation about gamers*
- *aggressive behaviour caused by other factors*
- *video games must be used wisely*

Video games – popular but dangerous?

Since they first appeared on the market in the 1970s and 1980s, arcade video games, gaming consoles and home computer games have come a long way. It is estimated that in Germany alone more than 30 million people over 14 play digital games regularly. Gamescom, the trade fair for video games, attracts several hundred thousand visitors every year. Despite these impressive figures and trends, controversy surrounding video and computer games has always accompanied the development and rise of this part of today's entertainment industry.
Many educators oppose computer games, arguing that devotees spend too much time in front of the computer screen. The addiction factor of the games could make students and adults neglect their duties, friends and families. In this way, excessive game-playing can lead to social isolation. The lack of communication may eventually result in the deterioration of reading, writing and speaking skills. Another serious and frequently repeated argument against video games is the suspicion that gamers, especially younger people, may become more aggressive and violent. Following any horrific mass shooting, sections of the population, politicians and educators maintain that digital games promote violent and anti-social behaviour. They

uphold that children are particularly vulnerable to the effects of media violence because they are often unable to distinguish between fantasy and reality. Consequently, in the view of many psychologists, violent computer games could induce brutality and lack of empathy. When players have to shoot others to stay alive, they will eventually lack moral scruples and react with indifference to real people's suffering. Respect and compassion for human beings gets lost. If the worst comes to the worst, excessive playing of such games may eventually turn teens into killers. To prevent this from happening these games should therefore be banned.

On the other hand, there are people who believe that these assumptions and demands are unfair, because they are generalising and unfounded. Fans argue that gamers and games have changed. Manufacturers of video games have begun to place warning labels on packages of violent content, such as M for Mature or AO for Adults Only, to restrict sale to adults. This may not be the ideal solution, but it is a first step at least. In addition, games have undergone a profound development and have changed in several ways. The ego shooters of the early years have been replaced by more sophisticated games which require players to be patient and cautious rather than aggressive and violent. In fact, players lose points for using too much violence and are rewarded when they succeed in completing a mission wisely and quietly. Furthermore, the image of the typical video gamer as a pasty faced, rather lazy and slightly maladjusted teenager is not the norm. Users come from all walks of life, and video gaming has become an accepted activity in people's free time. There are studies, albeit not completely undisputed, which suggest that video gaming promotes concentration, stamina and strategic skills. This is to say, the more elaborate games are exercises for the brain, because gamers have to analyse situations and find solutions for various tasks to get to the next level. One study even found that students who played online games regularly achieved better marks in maths and reading tests. Online games can also promote 'spatial ability', which is the capacity to understand and remember the relations between objects in a room or certain space. This faculty is needed in everyday life, such as when reading a map, for example.

All in all, I believe the question of whether video gaming has a negative impact depends on the nature of the game played and the player. I think everybody would agree that not all gamers turn into serial killers. The aggressive behaviour of some people is often the result of personal or family problems. However, there is the danger that anti-social attitudes could be intensified through the excessive consumption of violent computer games. The fact remains that video gaming is extremely popular and the production of online and video games is a highly profitable business.

(678 words)

Klausur 6: The Media

Leseverstehen 60 min.

Text 1: Does quitting social media make you happier?

Teenagers and young adults switching off from Facebook and other social apps reveal how the change has affected their lives.

Daisy, 23: […] Facebook made me feel anxious, depressed and like a failure. When I went online it seemed like everyone was in Australia or Thailand, and if they weren't travelling they were getting engaged or landing great jobs. I felt like everyone was living the dream and I was still at home with my parents, with debt from my student loan hanging over me. […]

Ben, 21: […] I'm in a much more positive mindset without social media than I ever was with it. It's let me see who my friends truly are, and who I was only concerned with simply because they were there on social media. I now use a basic non-smartphone and email as my only forms of communication, and people have adjusted to it. […]

Rosanna, 25: […] without Facebook I feel much happier and more content. I can live my life instead of trying to shape it into one that looks good online. I also have a lot more time now, and it's easy enough to keep in touch with my friends in other ways. What's more, now we can have conversations about what we've been doing because we haven't seen it all already on social media. […]

Kevin, 23: […] Leaving Facebook was one of the best decisions I've made this year. Aside from the increased productivity that comes from not having it, I enjoy actually talking to people face to face, and not seeing what someone I met once, years ago, had for breakfast. I do, however, forget to wish a lot of people happy birthday and I seem to be months behind in finding out some news – but I find out eventually.

Sophie, 18: […] I've been free from the chains of social media for about six months now, which doesn't seem like a lot of time, but it feels like it now that my time isn't being sapped by these apps. It sounds so silly, but since leaving I feel like my own person. Before, Facebook and Twitter became almost like extra arms attached to me that I constantly had to be aware of. I used to check for updates countless times every day. […]

Task 1

Read the comments carefully. Then match a suitable statement (1–7) to each one. There are more statements than you need. Write the number of the statement (1–7) below the person's name in the table. *(5)*

1 I do more socialising now.

2 I don't pretend anymore!

3 I don't feel lonely anymore.

4 I miss some things, though.

5 I'm in control of my life again.

6 I feel less under pressure.

7 Now I can concentrate on my true friends.

Daisy	Ben	Rosanna	Kevin	Sophie

Text 2: More digital disruption ahead for mainstream news groups, says survey

Traditional news outlets are facing a new wave of disruption as the digital revolution sweeps on, according to a new international survey.

It is likely to further change the relationship between news companies and their audiences and could have profound implications for societies in advanced economies.

According to the third annual digital news report published by the Reuters Institute for the Study of Journalism (RISJ), some news organisations are being outpaced by the speed of change while others show signs of rising to the challenge.

The report, in pointing to new threats to traditional news sources, identifies the smartphone and social media as the most powerful agents of change. It also reveals a clear generational split in how people are both finding and interpreting news. [...]

Meanwhile, the adoption of new technology is segmenting the news market. Smartphones, which are favoured by young people, are encouraging users to consume news more frequently throughout the day, thereby reducing the dependence on appointment-to-view television and printed newspaper issues.

The readers and viewers of tomorrow prefer to receive news through mobile devices and consequently tend to "snack" more in terms of both the time spent on sites and the type of content they consume.

Significantly, across all 10 countries surveyed by YouGov on behalf of the Reuters Institute, 36 % of 18–24s say they use smartphones as their primary access for news.

The report suggests that as this trend increases, different groups will develop their own, narrow relationship with news sources rather than sharing a broader range of views.

One of its editors, Nic Newman, says: "Across the world we see a generational split in terms of platforms, formats and the type of emerging news brands that are being consumed." […] *(296 words)*

© Roy Greenslade, 12. 06. 2014, https://www.theguardian.com/media/greenslade/2014/jun/12/digital-media-social-media

Annotation

l. 18 YouGov an international online market research organisation

Task 2

Complete each sentence using <u>no more than five words</u> from the text. *(8)*

1. Traditional media are challenged by ____________________.
2. ______________________________ will be most affected by this process.
3. There are different reactions to the new development; some providers of news find it hard to adapt to the changes but others are

   ______________________________.
4. ______________________________ differs between the young and the old.
5. Smartphones allow people to look at the news ______________

   ______________________________.
6. The move away from traditional news sources means people prefer to

   ________________ on information whenever they feel like it.
7. Smartphones are young adults' ____________________.
8. People are in danger of losing ____________________ because of their choice of news sources.

Text 3: Last reporters leave Fleet Street, ending centuries of journalism on the famous road

Fleet Street was once considered the most important location for journalism in the world, with Britain's national newspapers making the street their home for centuries.

The tightly-knit network of alleys and backstreets around Fleet Street became the embodiment of the British Press, and was notorious as much for the bustling offices full of <u>hacks</u> as it was for the numerous smoky bars frequented by them.

But since the 1980s, the street's era as a hub for journalism in the UK has waned and now the last two journalists working on the street are set to leave. […]

Fleet Street, or the "Street of Shame", as it is known by many, has been home to publishers since the 16th century, and London's first daily newspaper, *The Daily Courant*, was published there in 1702.

By the 20th century, Fleet Street as a national and international centre for journalism had been cemented, and was captured in its pomp in Evelyn Waugh's 1938 satirical novel *Scoop* in which unscrupulous authoritarian editors battle for prominence as their writers drink heavily in bars.

But Fleet Street's demise began in 1986 when Rupert Murdoch moved publication of his News International titles *The Times*, *News of the World* and *The Sun* to new premises in Wapping. Despite furious opposition from print unions, all of Mr Murdoch's Fleet Street print staff were sacked, thereby breaking the power of the unions, and electronic printing began in Wapping.

The following year, the *Telegraph* left its mock-Egyptian tower for Canary Wharf and the *Financial Times* moved out of Bracken House near St. Paul's Cathedral, crossing the river to Southwark.

In 1988, the *Daily Mail* made the move to west London, removing Lord Rothermere's original boardroom and relocating it to offices in Kensington.

In 1989 the *Express* left its spectacular art-deco offices on Fleet Street for Blackfriars Road.

But though all the journalists may now be gone, Fleet Street's legacy lives on, as a byword for the UK's national newspapers. *(339 words)*

Annotation

l. 5 hack a negative term for a journalist who writes low quality articles

Task 3

Read the text carefully. Tick (✓) the correct ending to each statement. *(6)*

1. Fleet Street used to be …
   - ☐ a bustling nightlife district.
   - ☐ the centre of British journalism.
   - ☐ the embodiment of British politics.
2. The newspaper offices were located …
   - ☐ along Fleet Street.
   - ☐ in the area of Fleet Street.
   - ☐ often above the Fleet Street bars.

3. In a book, Fleet Street was portrayed …
   - [ ] in a realistic way.
   - [ ] in a positive way.
   - [ ] rather unfavourably.

4. Rupert Murdoch's relocation of his news titles …
   - [ ] strengthened the power of the unions.
   - [ ] created a lot of new jobs.
   - [ ] brought about a major change in the industry.

5. Some newspaper headquarters …
   - [ ] stayed empty after the companies had moved.
   - [ ] are now no longer in Wapping.
   - [ ] had impressive offices.

6. Fleet Street …
   - [ ] is still associated with its past.
   - [ ] has become a synonym for the end of an era.
   - [ ] will soon be forgotten.

Textaufgabe 60 min.

Text: The future of the media

[…] It takes a brave man to put their head above the parapet and predict the future of media, especially when you consider the extraordinary and unpredictable explosion of technology that has both scarred and energised the industry in recent years. The tools and channels we now take for granted – Kindle, tablets, Twitter, Snapchat, Netflix, streaming, paywalls – were certainly not part of media veteran Torin Douglas's vernacular for much of his 24-year stint as the BBC's media correspondent.

So if things are changing with such rapidity, how can he – and other people – make accurate predictions about where we're headed?

"I believe that the future of the media is extremely healthy," says Torin who, after retiring from the BBC in 2013, now spends his days speaking, writing and chairing events. "We are, after all, living in one of its most exciting phases. Consistently over the past decades it has reinvented itself, yet all the while ensuring that creativity remains at the core. And the devices – whether on paper or screen or mobile – are all, in their own ways, robust. Not impervious but definitely robust. It would take a very courageous, or foolish, analyst indeed to predict the demise of any of them." […]

"There has been so much change in television alone that it's almost impossible to predict where we will be next year – let alone in decades to come," says Torin. "But this wave of multi-channel disruption that we're seeing, particularly from American companies, is evidence that TV is far more resilient than many imagined even a few years ago. The days of programmes pulling in 20 million viewers may have ended due to fragmentation but the traditional TV industry is incredibly strong."

Indeed. Who would have thought that Saturday night viewing – complete with singing and dancing competitions, chat shows and grandparent-friendly presenters – would still be the quintessential family moment of the week? And such a money-spinner for advertisers. Torin agrees: "Old-fashioned entertainment, no matter what the device that it's viewed on, is as vital and popular now as it ever was. Yes, *X Factor* pulls in fewer viewers – but seven or eight million a week is still an astonishing amount, considering the competition it has.

"And rather than merely eat into their share of the audience, new media is enhancing that television experience. Twitter is bringing people to the box in the corner of the room, encouraging them to be part of live 'conversations'. Television has morphed from a pure viewing experience into a participatory one and, one could argue, a far more fulfilling one. And this trend can only continue, enriching rather than disrupting the time we spend in front of our TVs." [...]

"[...] around seven million national papers are sold and read every day in Britain. Still. And that's not counting the consumption of local and free titles. There may be some consolidation in the years to come but we are not seeing the catastrophic implosion that some doom-mongers predicted. TV is not dead and neither are newspapers – if anything, the digital age has made them better, more relevant, more connected to an audience and more competitive. In that respect, the future is rosy."

The same is true for books, he says. In an age of momentary pleasures derived from YouTube videos, shallow blogs and instantly-disposable tweets, longform reading is more valuable than ever. Again, the business model has suffered considerably in the past few years but the more publishers engage with digital technology, the more secure their future will be. *(585 words)*

Annotation

l. 5 Torin Douglas media correspondent for the BBC from 1989–2013

Material: Cartoon

"Where did it all go wrong?"

Tasks

1. Outline Torin Douglas's attitude towards modern digital media. *(10)*
2. Comment on Torin Douglas's belief that "the future of the media is extremely healthy" (l. 9) by responding to the information in the text. *(20)*
3. Describe the cartoon and compare it to the belief held by Torin Douglas. *(30)*

Lösungsvorschläge

Leseverstehen

Task 1

Hinweis: *Statement 6: Daisy – "Facebook made me feel anxious, depressed and like a failure … I felt like everyone was living the dream …": There was pressure on Daisy to be like other people: they were having fun, and her life was not like that. Leaving Facebook, she broke away from that external pressure.*
Statement 7: Ben – "It's let me see who my friends truly are, and who I was only concerned with simply because they were there on social media.": Ben realised after quitting social media that there was a difference between true and social media friends.
Statement 2: Rosanna – "I can live my life instead of trying to shape it into one that looks good online.": Rosanna shows that her online image was not her true one. Now that she no longer uses social media, she can simply be herself with her friends.
Statement 1: Kevin – "… I enjoy actually talking to people face to face …": Kevin suggests that he is socialising more rather than just chatting digitally.
Statement 5: Sophie – "I've been free from the chains of social media …"/"… my time isn't being sapped by these apps."/"… since leaving I feel like my own person."/ "Before, Facebook and Twitter became almost like extra arms attached to me …": Sophie was dependent on social media, and she now feels that she is in charge of her life again and not that social media is ruling it.

Daisy	Ben	Rosanna	Kevin	Sophie
6	7	2	1	5

Task 2

Hinweis: *zu 1: "More digital disruption ahead for mainstream news groups …" (title) "Traditional news outlets are facing a new wave of disruption as the digital revolution sweeps on …" (ll. 1/2);*
zu 2: "… profound implications for societies in advanced economies." (l. 4)
zu 3: "… some news organisations are being outpaced by the speed of change while others show signs of rising to the challenge." (ll. 6/7)
zu 4: "… clear generational split in how people are both finding and interpreting news." (l. 10) / "… the adoption of new technology is segmenting the news market. Smartphones, which are favoured by young people, …" (ll. 11/12)
zu 5: "Smartphones … are encouraging users to consume news more frequently throughout the day, …" (ll. 11–13)
zu 6: "The readers and viewers of tomorrow prefer to receive news through mobile devices and consequently tend to "snack" more in terms of both the time spent on sites and the type of content they consume." (ll. 15–17)
zu 7: "… 36 % of 18–24s … smartphones as … primary access for news." (l. 19)

zu 8: "… different groups will develop their own, narrow relationship with news sources rather than sharing a broader range of views." (ll. 20–22)

1. Traditional media are challenged by **the digital revolution/digital disruption**.
2. **Societies in advanced economies** will be most affected by this process.
3. There are different reactions to the new development; some providers of news find it hard to adapt to the changes but others are **rising to the challenge**.
4. **Finding and interpreting news/The adoption of new technology** differs between the young and the old.
5. Smartphones allow people to look at the news **more frequently throughout the day**.
6. The move away from traditional news sources means people prefer to "**snack**" on information whenever they feel like it.
7. Smartphones are young adults' **primary access for news**.
8. People are in danger of losing **a broader range of views** because of their choice of news sources.

Task 3

Hinweis: *zu 1: title: "Last reporters leave Fleet Street …"; "Fleet Street was once considered the most important location for journalism in the world, with Britain's national newspapers making the street their home for centuries." (ll. 1/2)*
zu 2: "The tightly-knit network of alleys and backstreets around Fleet Street became the embodiment of the British Press …" (ll. 3/4)
zu 3: "… Fleet Street … was captured in its pomp in Evelyn Waugh's 1938 satirical novel Scoop *in which unscrupulous authoritarian editors battle for prominence as their writers drink heavily in bars." (ll. 11–14)*
zu 4: "Despite furious opposition from print unions, all of Mr Murdoch's Fleet Street print staff were sacked, thereby breaking the power of the unions, and electronic printing began in Wapping." (ll. 17–19)
zu 5: "… the Telegraph left its mock-Egyptian tower …" (l. 20)/"… the Express left its spectacular art-deco offices on Fleet Street …" (l. 25)
zu 6: "But though all the journalists may now be gone, Fleet Street's legacy lives on, as a byword for the UK's national newspapers." (ll. 27/28)

1. Fleet Street used to be …

   ☐ a bustling nightlife district.
   ☑ the centre of British journalism.
   ☐ the embodiment of British politics.

2. The newspaper offices were located …
   - [ ] along Fleet Street.
   - [x] in the area of Fleet Street.
   - [ ] often above the Fleet Street bars.

3. In a book, Fleet Street was portrayed …
   - [ ] in a realistic way.
   - [ ] in a positive way.
   - [x] rather unfavourably.

4. Rupert Murdoch's relocation of his news titles …
   - [ ] strengthened the power of the unions.
   - [ ] created a lot of new jobs.
   - [x] brought about a major change in the industry.

5. Some newspaper headquarters …
   - [ ] stayed empty after the companies had moved.
   - [ ] are now no longer in Wapping.
   - [x] had impressive offices.

6. Fleet Street …
   - [x] is still associated with its past.
   - [ ] has become a synonym for the end of an era.
   - [ ] will soon be forgotten.

Textaufgabe

1. ***Hinweis:*** *The key points are:*
   - *Douglas sees all forms of media as "robust" (ll. 13/14). He does not consider digital media to damage TV in spite of the huge selection of alternatives on offer (ll. 17–20).*
   - *Digital media has added value to television because of the aspect of participation it offers (ll. 29–34). Douglas believes that digital technology has brought television and its viewers – and also newspapers and their readers – closer together, making them more relevant.*
   - *He is therefore positive about the new developments (ll. 35–40).*
   - *The shallowness of social media will make people return to books; however, publishers must adapt to digital technology (ll. 41–45).*

   Basically, Torin Douglas does not believe that digital media should be looked upon negatively. In fact, he holds the view that traditional media should embrace the new

digital developments and build upon what they can offer. He considers that there is a role for every form of media to play and that each is fundamentally strong.
Turning to television as an example, he explains how in spite of a huge number of alternative channels on offer, modern media has not killed off the traditional TV providers. He acknowledges that viewer figures for individual programmes are lower than before but modern media have meant that viewers can now participate in programmes through 'live' conversations via Twitter, for example. He therefore sees modern media's influence on television programmes as being positive. Newspapers have benefited from modern technology in the same way as television by offering its readers the opportunity to participate in their news reporting and analysis.
Social media could be accused of being shallow, including the superficiality of many YouTube videos. However, Douglas sees this as being positive since many people will consequently seek material with more depth in content. As long as publishers turn to digital technology, reading books will not die out. *(203 words)*

2. ***Hinweis:*** *Here, you have to comment on Torin Douglas's opinion as stated in the article. Take Douglas's arguments and give your own view, which means that you can also use your own knowledge and experience.*

The article draws attention to the fact that there has been an "extraordinary and unpredictable explosion of technology" (ll. 2/3), which has hurt and influenced the media industry. The speed of change makes predictions difficult and doing this could therefore be seen as rather bold.
Many things based upon digital technology, such as Kindle and Twitter, are already accepted as mainstream, and although Torin Douglas sees developments such as these as opening up new opportunities, it is, however, up to the traditional media to respond to the digital revolution in a positive way, but it is not certain whether they will adapt sufficiently to succeed. In the case of TV programmes, which are now often geared to what the public want, the question is whether they are leading the way or responding to competition from the new media. Douglas avoids addressing this issue but says that TV entertainment is still alive. His optimism here is questionable as viewing figures for TV shows have been declining.
Similarly, he still sees the newspaper business as thriving, and criticises the "doommongers" (l. 38). However, seven million national newspapers sold each day is not a convincing statistic to prove that newspapers have a rosy future.
The interaction of the traditional media with new media may keep newspapers, books and television alive. This development has been going on for some years now, but it cannot be said for certain whether this is the right way for the future. Torin Douglas is very positive about the future of traditional media, but fails to address the question of whether this dual system will continue. All in all, I think his outlook for the traditional media is too optimistic, as digital media are becoming the main source of information and entertainment. *(289 words)*

3. ***Hinweis:*** *Here, your task is first to describe – and interpret – the cartoon, and then compare it with Torin Douglas's completely different view as quoted in the text.*

The cartoon shows two former newspaper employees, a photographer and a reporter, sitting on a pavement with their backs to a wall, which in itself is a symbolic image. The photographer looks very like a tramp with a torn and patched jacket. He is bearded and generally appears untidy and dirty. He is holding a sign which reads 'Please give'. In front of him on the pavement is a plate for collecting money from passers-by; in it are a couple of coins.
The journalist is also very scruffy, with worn out clothes, but he is still wearing a shirt and tie as if he has just had a bad day at the office; however, his collar is unbuttoned and his tie is hanging loosely around his neck.
The cartoonist has provided both figures with the tools of their trade – a camera for the photographer and a notepad for the reporter. In addition, the reporter has a pen behind his ear as used to be shown in clichéd images.
Next to the two men is a newspaper billboard with the headline of the fictitious 'Daily News' stating 'Read it free online'. The reporter asks the photographer where everything went wrong.
The image portrays the demise of the traditional newspaper as a result of the internet and free online news, and also how newspaper employees will consequently be made redundant and will no longer be required by the modern world.
The cartoon contradicts the media belief held by Torin Douglas in the text. Douglas considers the newspaper industry to be healthy and responding well to changes. He states that the doom-mongering – which the cartoon portrays – is unjustified and false. In fact, he believes that new technology has actually benefited the industry.
The cartoon and the text portray two differing pictures of the effect digital technology will have on the future of the media – only time will tell which one is correct.

(319 words)

Klausur 7: The American Dream

Leseverstehen 30 min.

Text 1: Why the Working Poor Believe in the American Dream

The Harrisons had clearly not benefited from the intended trickle-down effect of the administration's tax cuts. They had no private health insurance but, because of Tom's job as a truck driver, they were too well off to qualify for Medicare. Like tens of millions of Americans, they were the working poor, who fell between two stools. […]

In Europe Gene [Harrison] and her family wouldn't just have been eligible for state welfare; they would also happily have described themselves as poor or at least working class. "The middle classes is hurting," she told me with the heavy, short breath of the morbidly obese.

"You don't think of yourself as working class?" Gene looked at me as if I was deranged. "No, honey," she said, "we are working *people*. Oh yes. But we are definitely middle class!" For Gene and her family the American dream was in reality a farce verging on a nightmare. But the dream of prosperity, of endless opportunity, is a stubborn one. This explains why the majority of lower-income Americans oppose scrapping tax cuts for the rich. As an economist in Ohio once explained to me: "We all think that we might be rich one day. To put the rich in another bracket is an acknowledgement that we'll never get there!" […]

This is particularly fascinating because the statistics flesh out what can only be described as a growing gap between perception and reality. A *New York Times* survey in 2007 indicated that 45 per cent of those polled believe they were better off than they were at birth, even though the facts show that is not the case. The fact is that every survey shows a widening gulf between rich and poor. According to the Congressional Budget Office the top income of the top one per cent of Americans jumped a 139 per cent between 1979 and 2001 to an average of more than $ 700,000 a year. The income of the middle fifth rose by just 17 per cent in the same period to a mere $ 43,700, and for the bottom fifth it was just 9 per cent, well below the level of inflation. The rich are getting far richer. The poor are staying poor. Every statistic tells the same story. At America's top 250 colleges the proportion of children from top-income families has grown, not shrunk. Poverty breeds continuity. The average age for women without college education to have their first child is 22, just as it was in the early 1970s. The average for women with a college education has gone from 25 to 30. Educated women have careers. Uneducated ones still do not.

In terms of income and education American society is surprisingly immobile. What masks the disparity is that cheap labour and mass production have enabled even the poor to enjoy the trappings of affluence. Both of Gene's sons have iPods. She has a small flat-screen TV.

Between them they own three cars. They all have mobile phones. But their diet is cheap and potentially deadly. Their health is woeful and their life expectancy is not much higher than it would have been for a similar family fifty years ago. And yet they feel constitutionally optimistic. They have an inalienable right to dream of a better life even if reality dictates that they will never achieve it. It is one of the great blessings of the American political system. In this country the poor still think they are princes-in-waiting. Ever since Benjamin Franklin rose to greatness as one of seventeen children of a humble candle-maker, Americans have fallen in love with the rags-to-riches journey. Politics continues to dish up enough examples to keep the dream alive. Bill Clinton, the man from Hope (Arkansas), was brought up by a poor, single mother. Senator John Edwards made his fortune as a trial lawyer defending the kind of Americans he grew up with. He adopted a firebrand message about the "shameful division of the two Americas" while never apologizing for his own wealth or skimping on his expensive haircuts. In Europe he might have been reviled as a hypocrite. In America he embodied the dream. *(692 words)*

Annotations

l. 1	trickle-down effect	belief that additional wealth gained by the richest people in society will have a positive economic effect on the lives of everyone because the rich will invest their extra money
l. 3	Medicare and Medicaid	government programmes that provide medical and health-related services to specific groups of people in the United States
l. 5	eligible	meeting the necessary conditions
l. 12	to verge on sth	to be very close to sth
l. 15	bracket	here: group
l. 33	disparity	inequality
l. 34	trapping	possession, characteristic
l. 39	inalienable right	a right that cannot be taken from you
l. 42	Benjamin Franklin	(1706–1790); one of the Founding Fathers of the United States, inventor, author, statesman
ll. 44/45	Bill Clinton	42nd President of the United States (1993–2001)
l. 46	John Edwards	former US senator, candidate for the Democratic presidential nomination in 2004 and 2008
l. 49	to revile	to criticise
l. 49	hypocrite	someone who pretends to have certain beliefs or opinions that he/she does not live up to

Tasks *(10)*

- Tick the correct statement(s) or give short answers.
- Use a quotation from the text to support each correct statement

1. The Harrisons could not participate in the state-subsidised health insurance programme because they *(1)*

   ☐ were too poor.

   ☐ were unemployed.

   ☐ were too affluent.

   ☐ had a criminal record.

   line(s) ______: ____

   ____

2. Most poor Americans are in favour of taxing rich people more heavily. *(1)*

   ☐ true

   ☐ false

   line(s) ______: ____

   ____

3. Statistics prove that forty-five per cent of Americans are wealthier than they were when they were born. *(1)*

   ☐ true

   ☐ false

   line(s) ______: ____

   ____

4. In the 1980s and 1990s, the rate of inflation was higher than the income growth of the bottom twenty per cent of the American population. *(1)*

   ☐ true

   ☐ false

   line(s) ______: ____

   ____

5. Widespread consumerism even among the lower social classes camouflages the lack of social mobility in American society. *(1)*

   ☐ true ☐ false

   line(s) ______: ____

   ____

6. Which is the major reason for the Harrisons' ill health? *(1)*
   - ☐ excessive use of modern technology
   - ☐ poor education
   - ☐ inadequate nutrition
   - ☐ lack of physical exercise

   line(s) ______ : ____

   ____

7. Explain the sentence "In this country, the poor still think they are princes-in waiting." (ll. 41/42) *(2)*

   ____

   ____

   ____

   ____

   ____

8. Explain why John Edwards's actions can be considered hypocritical. *(2)*

   ____

   ____

   ____

   ____

   ____

Analyse/Sprachmittlung 60 min.

Text 2: Der amerikanische Traum hat Dellen bekommen

Schaut man auf die Zahl der illegalen Einwanderer im Land, dann hat der amerikanische Traum nichts von seiner Anziehungskraft eingebüßt. Noch immer kommen Arme und Aufstiegswillige besonders aus Südamerika, um in Amerika ihr Glück zu suchen. Allein im Lande selbst verliert der American Dream seit Jahren an Leuchtkraft. […]

Die Mittelschicht in Amerika von links bis rechts ist unzufrieden und zukunftsskeptisch geworden. […] Seit den 90er-Jahren sind die Löhne nicht gestiegen, selbst das […] Wirtschaftswachstum hat sich bisher noch nicht in den Geldbeuteln niedergeschlagen. […] Überhaupt ist der Traum vom Aufstieg von vielen Studien entzaubert worden. Demnach bieten inzwischen manche Länder in West- und Nordeuropa bessere Chancen, sich von unten nach oben hochzuarbeiten – Deutschland eingeschlossen. Ist der amerikanische Traum also ausgeträumt?

Um dieser Frage auf den Grund zu gehen, geht man am besten zu Karlyn Bowman […]. Bowman ist die Umfrageexpertin [eines] konservativen Thinktanks […]. „Die Leute definieren den Traum sehr persönlich", sagt Bowman. Seit den 1980ern haben sich die Kriterien dafür kaum verändert. Weiterkommen durch Bildung und harte Arbeit, ein Haus zu besitzen und dass es die Kinder einmal besser haben sollen als man selbst, das sind die Konstanten.

Doch gerade die Zukunftshoffnung hat in den Krisenjahren stark abgenommen. Viele glauben nicht mehr daran, dass Amerika das Land unbegrenzter Möglichkeiten ist. Im Jahr 1952 beantworteten noch 87 Prozent die Frage, ob es reichlich Chancen in Amerika gebe, mit Ja. Seitdem ist die Zahl kontinuierlich gesunken, im Jahr 2013 glaubten daran nur noch 52 Prozent. Und selbst wenn harte Arbeit immer noch ein sehr wichtiger Wert für Amerikaner ist, so meinen doch immer weniger von ihnen, dass diese harte Arbeit auch belohnt wird. […]

„Der Finanzcrash hatte einen enormen Einfluss auf Amerika", sagt Bowman. „Angst ist normalerweise kein Gefühl, das man in Meinungsumfragen besonders oft registriert, aber wir sahen ziemlich deutlich, dass die Menschen 2008 und 2009 fürchteten, das Wirtschaftssystem könne zusammenbrechen." Seitdem sind die Bürger sehr pessimistisch, bis heute. […]

Dabei sind die Ansprüche, die die Leute an ihren „Traum" stellen, relativ bescheiden. Sie entsprechen auch nicht dem europäischen Klischee von den nur auf Geld und materiellen Gewinn ausgerichteten Amerikanern. Zwar steht das eigene Haus als Ziel weit oben, weil man den Kindern etwas vererben will. Aber ansonsten rangieren Dinge wie „Reichtum" oder „sich alles kaufen zu können, was man möchte" ganz unten auf der Skala der Dinge, die die Amerikaner mit ihrem Traum verbinden. […]

Die Amerikaner sind auch erstaunlich realistisch in finanziellen Dingen. Wenn man sie fragt, wie viel sie brauchten, um gerade so durchzukommen, dann stimmen die Antworten in etwa mit der definierten Armutsgrenze überein. Fragt man nach dem, was nötig ist, um einigermaßen komfortabel zu leben, antworten sie meistens mit einem Gehalt, das im Bereich des mittleren Einkommens in den USA liegt. Und um sich alle Träume zu erfüllen, reichen nach Antwort der meisten Amerikaner zwischen 100 000 und 200 000 Dollar im Jahr. Das sind nicht gerade überzogene Ansprüche. Und doch haben viele Bürger das Gefühl, es laufe etwas fundamental falsch im Land der unbegrenzten Möglichkeiten.

Amerikaner haben immer an Bildung als Mittel zum Aufstieg geglaubt. Früher wollten sie, dass ihre Söhne und Töchter die Highschool absolvieren und eine Chance haben, aufs College zu kommen. Heute hoffen sie, dass der Nachwuchs das College absolviert und eine Chance auf ein weiterführendes Studium hat. Doch die Uni-Gebühren sind in den vergangenen Jahrzehnten geradezu explodiert, während die mittleren Einkommen stagnierten. Und das öffentliche Schulsystem scheint kaum noch in der Lage, die Unterschiede in den Startchancen der Schüler auszugleichen, damit auch Kinder aus unterprivilegierten Haushalten eine Chance bekommen. […]

Irgendwann in den vergangenen Jahren ist den sonst so optimistischen Amerikanern der Glaube an die Zukunft verloren gegangen. Seit Anfang 2000 ist die Hoffnung der Jungen, dass es ihnen einmal bessergehen wird als ihren Eltern, von 72 auf 42 Prozent gesunken. Ihre Eltern sind noch pessimistischer. Nur 20 Prozent glauben, ihre Kinder hätten heute bessere Chancen, als sie selbst einst hatten. […]

Aber das Bild ist eben nicht nur düster, es weist auch Grauschattierungen auf. So rangiert die Zahl derjenigen, die für sich sagen, den Traum schon verwirklicht zu haben, stabil zwischen 30 und 40 Prozent. Diese Zahl ist bei den oft zur Unterschicht gehörenden Hispanics und den Schwarzen […] geringer (im Jahr 2013 je 30 und 21 Prozent). Dafür glauben aber 56 Prozent der Hispanics und 60 Prozent der Schwarzen, die noch nicht am Ziel ihrer Träume angekommen sind, dass sie ihren persönlichen amerikanischen Traum irgendwann erreichen werden. „Der amerikanische Traum ist lädiert und angeschlagen“, sagt Bowman, „aber er ist immer noch lebendig.“

(755 words)

Clemens Wergin, 20. 01. 2015, https://www.welt.de/politik/ausland/article136548431/Der-amerikanische-Traum-hat-Dellen-bekommen.html

Task

You are participating in a massive open online course (MOOC) offered by the German-American Institute (DAI) in Heidelberg. Each participant has to write a report on an aspect of American identity.
Your topic is the American Dream in the 21st century. You have to answer the question of whether Americans still believe in the American Dream.
Use Text 1 and Text 2. *(25)*

Lösungsvorschläge

Leseverstehen

1. The Harrisons could not participate in the state-subsidised health insurance programme because they
   - ☐ were too poor.
   - ☐ were unemployed.
   - ☑ were too affluent.
   - ☐ they had a criminal record.

   line **3: "they were too well off (to qualify for Medicare)."**

2. Most poor Americans are in favour of taxing rich people more heavily.
   - ☐ true
   - ☑ false

   lines **13/14: "the majority of lower-income Americans oppose scrapping tax cuts for the rich."**

3. Statistics prove that forty-five per cent of Americans are wealthier than they were when they were born.
   - ☐ true
   - ☑ false

   lines **19/20: "45 per cent (of those polled) believe they were better off than they were at birth, even though the facts show that is not the case."**

4. In the 1980s and 1990s, the rate of inflation was higher than the income growth of the bottom twenty per cent of the American population.
   - ☑ true
   - ☐ false

   lines **23–25: "between 1979 and 2001 … for the bottom fifth it was just 9 per cent, well below the level of inflation."**

5. Widespread consumerism even among the lower social classes camouflages the lack of social mobility in American society.
   - ☑ true
   - ☐ false

   lines **32–34: "What masks the disparity is that cheap labour and mass production have enabled even the poor to enjoy the trappings of affluence."**

6. Which is the major reason for the Harrisons' ill health?
   - [ ] excessive use of modern technology
   - [ ] poor education
   - [x] inadequate nutrition
   - [ ] lack of physical exercise

   lines **36/37: "their diet is cheap and potentially deadly. Their health is woeful"**

7. Explain the sentence "In this country, the poor still think they are princes-in waiting."
   Poor Americans still believe in the American Dream in the sense that everybody – even they – can go from rags to riches.

8. Explain why John Edwards's actions can be considered hypocritical.
   Although he publicly condemned inequality, he had an extravagant lifestyle.

Analyse/Sprachmittlung

***Hinweis:** This task requires you to use information from texts 1 and 2 to write your own text on the topic given. Do not translate the German text or take whole passages from the English text. Use your own words and focus only on the aspects relevant to the task. You are required to write within a specific context (here: MOOC) and for specific addressees (here: participants and teachers of MOOC). Make sure you use the text type the task requires (report).*

The American Dream is a defining concept of American national identity: the idea that you can achieve anything in your life if you work hard for it. Since the beginning of the 21st century, this concept has been challenged by globalisation and the financial and economic crisis starting in 2007. In view of this development, the question arises whether Americans in the 21st century still believe in the American Dream.
(In his book *Only in America*) Matt Frei suggests that the American Dream is still alive even among the lower classes of US society. As everybody still believes that they might strike it rich one day, even poorer people oppose taxing the rich more heavily in order to support the less fortunate – even though they might benefit from such measures themselves. Empirical data, however, suggest that this optimism might be unfounded. Several surveys have shown that the gap between rich and poor is widening. According to the Congressional Budget Office, the income of the top one per cent rose by 139 per cent in the years 1979 to 2001, whereas the income of the bottom twenty per cent only rose by nine per cent – which is lower than the level of inflation. Another fact that supports the idea that social mobility might be a mere dream is that the proportion of students from rich families at American universities has increased. According to Matt Frei, many Americans keep believing in the American Dream because these disparities are concealed by the fact that through mass production almost everyone, even families who belong to the working poor, can enjoy the blessings of a consumer society.

Clemens Wergin, the author of the article *Der amerikanische Traum hat Dellen bekommen*, which was published in 2015, makes slightly different observations. The Dream still draws many immigrants to the United States, but has lost its shine among Americans. The American middle class, regardless of political affiliations, has become dissatisfied and pessimistic about the future. Real wages have remained the same since the 1990s, and studies have shown that going from rags to riches is the exception rather than the rule in America. A survey shows that in 1952, 78 per cent of Americans believed that America was a land of opportunity, in 2013 only 52 per cent thought that this was the case. Wergin partly attributes this development to the financial and economic crisis, during which many Americans feared the economy might collapse altogether. This pessimism is even more surprising given the fact that most Americans do not dream of becoming the next Rockefeller; what they primarily have in mind is having a house and a moderate income. One reason why even this is out of reach for many Americans is that education, which has always been perceived as a key to success, fails to equalise social differences. That is why Americans are far less optimistic now than they used to be at the beginning of the 21st century. While in 2000 72 per cent of young Americans believed that one day they would be better off than their parents, in 2015 only 42 per cent were convinced that this was true. Yet, the reality is not as bleak as these figures suggest. The percentage of people who believe they have already realised the American Dream is quite stable and ranges between 30 and 40 per cent. That is why Karlyn Bowman, who works for a conservative think tank, comes to the conclusion that the American Dream is ailing but still alive.

All in all, both authors agree that American society has become more unequal over the past few decades and that people from lower classes are not very likely to work their way up. While Matt Frei found the Dream to be alive and well in 2008, less than a decade later, Clemens Wergin establishes that Americans have lost much of their optimism. It remains to be seen whether this is mainly due to the financial and economic crisis or whether it is a general trend. *(670 words)*

Klausur 8: Globalisation

Hör-/Sehverstehen 20 min.

▶ Video

Bolivia: Crazy for Quinoa

Read the tasks and items below, then watch the video and complete the tasks. Watch the video three times. *(30)*

1. Quinoa has been cultivated for centuries, but only recently has it become *(2)*

   ____.

2. Quinoa contains … *(1)*
   - ☐ a higher amount of protein and carbohydrates than many other grains.
   - ☐ fewer carbohydrates than many other grains.
   - ☐ less protein than corn.
   - ☐ more carbohydrates than rice and corn.

3. Where can you now purchase quinoa? Name two possibilities. *(2)*

   a) ____

   b) ____

4. In Bolivia, quinoa … *(1)*
   - ☐ is preferred to more nutritious imported grains.
   - ☐ has always been highly regarded because of its nutritional value.
   - ☐ has not been recognised for its benefits for a long time.
   - ☐ is less important than imported grains.

5. The CEO of Alexander Coffee believes that Bolivians … *(2)*

   ____.

6. Ms Quezada participated in a campaign to ____________________

   __________ which was supported by ____________________. *(2)*

7. Name two groups the programme involved. *(2)*

   a) ____

   b) ____

8. Name two facts about the quinoa chocolate chip cookies. *(2)*

a) ____

b) ____

9. According to Wilfredo Rojas, two steps have to be taken in order to guarantee product reliability. List them. *(2)*

a) ____

b) ____

10. As much of the production is destined for ____________________,

it is a challenge to find farmers who can produce ________________

____________________ needed for local businesses. *(4)*

11. Note down the altitude at which Elias Vargas and Viviana Herrera grow their quinoa. *(1)*

____

12. Name two ways in which project staff can help Viviana and Elias. *(2)*

a) ____

b) ____

13. Explain the consequences of the fact that farmers sell more quinoa now. *(3)*

____

____

Post-viewing task:

14. Summarise the film's message about quinoa in Bolivia. *(4)*

____

____

____

____

Textaufgabe 160 min.

Can vegans stomach the unpalatable truth about quinoa?

By Joanna Blythman

Not long ago, quinoa was just an obscure Peruvian grain you could only buy in wholefood shops. We struggled to pronounce it (it's keen-wa, not qui-no-a), yet it was <u>feted</u> by food lovers as a novel addition to the familiar ranks of couscous and rice. Dieticians <u>clucked</u> over quinoa approvingly because it ticked the low-fat box and fitted in with government healthy eating advice to "base your meals on <u>starch</u>y foods".

Adventurous eaters liked its slightly bitter taste and the little white curls that formed around the grains. Vegans embraced quinoa as a credibly nutritious substitute for meat. Unusual among grains, quinoa has a high protein content (between 14 %–18 %), and it contains all those pesky, yet essential, amino acids needed for good health that can prove so elusive to vegetarians who prefer not to pop food supplements.

Sales took off. Quinoa was, in marketing speak, the "miracle grain of the Andes", a healthy, right-on, ethical addition to the meat avoider's <u>larder</u> (no dead animals, just a crop that doesn't feel pain). Consequently, the price shot up – it has tripled since 2006 – with more rarified black, red and "royal" types commanding particularly handsome premiums.

But there is an unpalatable truth to face for those of us with a bag of quinoa in the larder. The appetite of countries such as ours for this grain has pushed up prices to such an extent that poorer people in Peru and Bolivia, for whom it was once a nourishing <u>staple food</u>, can no longer afford to eat it. Imported junk food is cheaper. In Lima, quinoa now costs more than chicken. Outside the cities, and fuelled by overseas demand, the pressure is on to turn land that once produced a portfolio of diverse crops into quinoa monoculture.

In fact, the quinoa trade is yet another troubling example of a damaging north-south exchange, with well-intentioned health and ethics-led consumers here <u>unwittingly</u> driving poverty there. It's beginning to look like a cautionary tale of how a focus on exporting premium foods can damage the producer country's food security. Feeding our apparently <u>insatiable</u> 365-day-a-year hunger for this luxury vegetable, Peru has also cornered the world market in asparagus. Result? In the arid Ica region where Peruvian asparagus production is concentrated, this thirsty export vegetable has depleted the water resources on which local people depend. NGOs report that asparagus labourers toil in sub-standard conditions and cannot afford to feed their children while <u>fat cat</u> exporters and foreign supermarkets cream off the profits. That's the <u>pedigree</u> of all those bunches of pricy spears on supermarket shelves.

Soya, a foodstuff beloved of the vegan lobby as an alternative to dairy products, is another problematic import, one that drives environmental destruction. Embarrassingly, for those who portray it as a progressive alternative to planet-destroying meat, soya production is now one of the two main causes of deforestation in South America, along with cattle ranching, where vast expanses of forest and grassland have been felled to make way for huge plantations.

Three years ago, the pioneering Fife Diet, Europe's biggest local food-eating project, sowed an experimental crop of quinoa. It failed, and the experiment has not been repeated. […]

In this respect, omnivores have it easy. Britain excels in producing meat and dairy foods for them to enjoy. However, a rummage through the shopping baskets of vegetarians and vegans swiftly clocks up the food miles, a consequence of their higher dependency on products imported from faraway places. […] *(577 words)*

Annotations

Heading:	unpalatable	distasteful
l. 2	to fete	to honour, to praise
l. 4	to cluck	noises hens typically make
l. 5	starchy	*stärkehaltig, auf Stärke basierend (ernährungswiss.)*
l. 12	larder	pantry
l. 19	staple food	*Haupt-/Grundnahrungsmittel*
l. 24	unwittingly	unintentionally
l. 27	insatiable	impossible to satisfy
l. 31	fat cat	big shot, leaders of huge enterprises
l. 32	pedigree	*here:* origin, background
l. 43	omnivore	creature that eats everything

Tasks

1. Outline the development of quinoa consumption and its effects. *(12)*
2. Analyse the strategies the author uses in order to make clear her view of the increasing consumption of quinoa. *(19)*
3. You have a choice here. Choose one task. *(17)*
   a) Write a dialogue in which a British vegan, a poor Bolivian mother of five, a Peruvian asparagus worker and the boss of an international food company discuss the consequences of globalised food production.

   or

   b) The publication of the article by Blythman triggered many responses. Peta (People for the Ethical Treatment of Animals) stated:
   "Eating quinoa may harm Bolivian farmers, but eating meat harms us all." Comment.

Lösungsvorschläge

Hör-/Sehverstehen

Transkript: Bolivia – Crazy for Quinoa

Narrator: Quinoa, cultivated for centuries in the Andean region, has become one of the world's trendiest new foods. With more protein and fewer carbohydrates than equal amounts of corn or rice, this member of the spinach family is now regularly sold in restaurants and health food stores in many countries. Yet here in Bolivia, the world's largest grower and exporter, quinoa has been looked down on in favor of less nutritious imported grains.

Pamy Quezada: At first, the mentality was that it was food for the poor people, but, in reality, I believe that in time we're beginning to understand that quinoa has many positive benefits.

Narrator: Four years ago, La Paz businesswoman Pamy Quezada began serving quinoa at her chain of restaurants. She was taking part in a campaign to promote quinoa in Bolivia. Supported by the UN's International Fund for Agricultural Development, the scheme not only involved local businesses but policymakers, marketing experts, farmers and research institute Bioversity International.

Pamy Quezada: It was hard at first, but now many people are opening up to quinoa and we're doing well, we're doing very well because of quinoa.

Narrator: One of her bestsellers is this quinoa chocolate chip cookie. Her company bakes more than 1,000 a day. Each one looks and tastes the same, and while that might not seem extraordinary one of the challenges for those working to promote quinoa has been to understand how to create products reliably.

Wilfredo Rojas: It is impossible to create the same product over and over again if you don't start from the same raw ingredients. That is why it is crucial to understand each variety of quinoa, and then link the business that needs that variety with the farmer who can produce it in small amounts.

Narrator: But with much of Bolivia's quinoa already destined for foreign markets, finding farmers who could produce specific varieties for local businesses was a challenge, which is why project staff came here to Lake Titicaca, 3,800 meters above sea level. Small farmers like Elias Vargas and Viviana Herrera have traditionally grown quinoa but were cut out of the international export market because the volumes they produced were too small. Now project staff are helping them identify specific quinoa varieties as well as forge links with local food stores, bakeries and restaurants who want to buy it.

Elias Vargas: Now people everywhere are buying quinoa. In the past, they were selling it in the markets. For that reason, we are able to sell our small quantities, and with that money we can support ourselves.

Narrator: Ironically, with more money to spend, families here are also beginning to eat more imported foods just like their city cousins, but here, too, helping them understand the nutritional benefits of eating quinoa as well as different ways to prepare it seems to be paying off.

Elias Vargas: Before, when we didn't know that quinoa was so healthy we sold it and bought noodles. Now that we know that quinoa is so good we don't buy other foods. Now we clean the quinoa and make soup out of it. We make juice, cakes, everything out of quinoa.

Narrator: There are more than three thousand varieties of quinoa found in the Andes, many capable of surviving extreme temperatures as well as high altitudes. Understanding the differences in these varieties will undoubtedly lead to increased consumption and a brighter future for these Andean farmers. *(570 words)*

Hinweis: *When doing the audio-visual test the following tips might help you.*
- *First, read the tasks carefully to be prepared for what is to come.*
- *In some tasks you will find words from the video. That does not necessarily mean that this item is the correct one.*
- *The tasks are in chronological order, so have a look at them from time to time while you are watching the video.*
- *Although many tasks can be answered by simply listening, there are some that you can only answer when actually viewing. You can recognise these tasks when there is a reference to a person who can only be identified by his/her name tag, or to a sign on a building, for example.*
- *When viewing for the first time try to answer as many tasks as possible.*
- *When viewing for the second and third time focus on the tasks you have not answered yet.*
- *The last task requires you to prove your general understanding of the text. Do this task after having viewed the video for the second time.*
- *Spelling and grammar are not assessed here, but make sure that one can understand what you want to say.*
- *Even if you think you have not understood a lot when viewing for the first time, you will discover that you have grasped more than you think.*

1. Quinoa has been cultivated for centuries, but only recently has it become **a trend food/one of the world's trendiest (new) foods**.

2. Quinoa contains …
   - ☐ a higher amount of protein and carbohydrates than many other grains.
   - ☑ less carbohydrates than many other grains.
   - ☐ less protein than corn.
   - ☐ more carbohydrates than rice and corn.

3. a) restaurants
   b) health food stores

4. In Bolivia, quinoa …
   - [ ] is preferred to more nutritious imported grains.
   - [ ] has always been highly regarded because of its nutritional value.
   - [x] has not been recognised for its benefits for a long time.
   - [ ] is less important than imported grains.
5. The CEO of Alexander Coffee believes that Bolivians **will begin to understand the (positive) benefits of quinoa/are opening up to quinoa.**
6. Ms Quezada participated in a campaign to **promote quinoa** which was supported by **the UN('s International Fund for Agricultural Development)**.
7. a) local businesses
   b) policymakers/marketing experts/farmers/a research institute
8. a) more than 1,000 cookies (are) baked every day
   b) they all look/taste the same
9. a) understand each variety of quinoa
   b) link farmer(s)/producer(s) and businesses
10. As much of the production is destined for **foreign markets**, it is a challenge to find farmers who can produce **specific varieties** needed for local businesses.
11. 3,800 m
12. a) identify specific quinoa varieties
    b) help to forge links with local businesses (food stores, bakeries and restaurants)
13. They can support themselves by earning more money, which makes them buy more imported food. However, they have also discovered the nutritional value of quinoa.
14. The film wants to convey the message that with the increasing export of quinoa the healthy grain is now beginning to gain more importance in Bolivia itself as farmers and institutions try to promote the cultivation, processing and consumption of quinoa for the home market.

Textaufgabe

1. ***Hinweis:*** *Outline how the consumption of quinoa has developed. It is not necessary to describe the nutritional qualities of quinoa in detail. Concentrate on the effects this development has. Information about other examples of agricultural globalisation need not be mentioned. Do not forget to write a sentence in which you introduce the topic.*
   - *Development:*
     - *Until recently: quinoa = relatively unknown*
     - *Purchase: only in specialised shops*
     - *Dieticians and government: promotion of nutritional benefits of quinoa → sales and prices skyrocketed*
   - *Effects:*
     - *People in poor countries of origin cannot afford quinoa anymore → eating cheaper, unhealthy food*
     - *Dependence on imported food*
     - *Cultivation of monocultures to satisfy quinoa demand*

   In her article "Can vegans stomach the unpalatable truth about quinoa?" published by *The Guardian*, author Joanna Blythman outlines the negative effects that a sharp increase in the consumption of quinoa in industrialised countries has on the people in the countries from which quinoa originates.
   Until recently, quinoa has been a relatively unknown grain from Peru which was only available in specialised food shops. However, since both dieticians and governments advocated its nutritional value and benefits, sales have surged among vegans and vegetarians. The increase in demand has caused the price of quinoa to skyrocket. As a consequence, quinoa – which has always been a staple food in Peru and Bolivia, for example, has become too expensive for poorer people to buy so that they have to resort to cheaper, imported food which does not have the nutritional qualities quinoa has. Moreover, due to the increasing demand, more and more fields have been turned into monocultures, destroying the diversity of crops. *(160 words)*

2. ***Hinweis:*** *In this task, you have to shift your focus from content to analysis. Although the task leaves you a certain amount of freedom, only speaking of "strategies the author uses", there is a range of devices you should take into account, such as structure, rhetorical devices and language/register. Before you start writing, make sure that you understand what the author thinks of the increasing consumption of quinoa.*
   - *Structure:*
     - *Introduction with reference to recent developments, main part, conclusion/ indirect appeal*
     - *Thesis at beginning of main part, introduced by "But", supported by arguments (junk food, monoculture), amplified by examples of asparagus and soya.*
     - *Conclusion: nutrition of the population in the producing countries is endan-*

gered; at the same time higher dependence of Western vegans/vegetarians on imported food
  - *Arguments supported by examples, figures, reference to organisations, but often remaining vague*
- *Rhetorical devices:*
  - *Irony (e. g. "obscure Peruvian grain", l. 1)*
  - *Figurative speech: "fat cat exporters" (l. 31), "cautionary tale" (l. 25), "planet-destroying meat" (l. 36), "rummage through the shopping baskets" (l. 44)*
  - *Antitheses: "appetite" vs. "nourishing staple food" (ll. 17–19), "here – there" (ll. 24/25), "cannot afford to feed their children while fat cat exporters ... cream off" (ll. 31/32)*
  - *Personifications: "appetite of countries" (l. 17), "pesky amino acids" (l. 9), "thirsty export vegetable" (l. 29)*
  - *Receiver-including pronouns: "We", "countries such as ours" (l. 17)*
- *Language/register:*
  - *Word field "food consumption": "adventurous eaters" (l. 6), "meat avoider" (l. 12), "vegetarians", "vegans", "well-intentioned ... consumers" (l. 24), "omnivores" (l. 43)*
  - *Technical terminology (e. g. "deforestation", l. 37) but text written in a clear and vivid style (e. g. "rummage through the shopping baskets")*

In her article, Joanna Blythman conveys her negative attitude towards the dramatically increased consumption of quinoa and the subsequent effects this has on the producing countries. To convince the reader of her point, Blythman uses a range of strategies, including structural and stylistic devices and register.
First of all, it can be said that Blythman structures her article in a way that is easy to follow. In her introduction (ll. 1–15) she informs the reader about the recent development regarding the consumption of quinoa. In order to make the change clear, she refers first to the past and then to the present. Signalling that a new part of her argument is about to begin ("But", l. 16), Blythman begins the main part (ll. 16–42) with the thesis that the rising consumption of quinoa in Western countries has severe consequences in the producing countries. She uses an antithesis to underline this connection: "The appetite of countries such as ours for this grain has pushed up prices to such an extent that poorer people in Peru and Bolivia, for whom it was once a nourishing staple food, can no longer afford to eat it" (ll. 17–19). She supports her thesis by presenting arguments such as stating that chicken or junk food are now cheaper than quinoa and that large areas of farmland are being turned into monocultures. The author reinforces her arguments by also referring to asparagus and soya in the following part. By giving them as further examples of the consequences the western "appetite" (l. 17) has on the producing countries is a clever way to draw the reader onto her side, as these two vegetables are well known – maybe in contrast to quinoa. In her conclusion (ll. 43–46), she points out two more

consequences of eating food from distant countries: high food miles and the dependence of vegetarians and vegans on imported food. She thus appeals to the reader to resort to homegrown food, including meat.

Blythman also uses a variety of rhetorical devices in order to make her point clear. One of the most striking strategies she uses throughout the text is irony. Right at the beginning of her article, Blythman speaks of "an obscure Peruvian grain" (l. 1), thus making fun of the ensuing hype around a grain which was once completely unknown in the West. Blythman also makes fun of herself and other Westerners when she states that quinoa was so strange and foreign that they could not even pronounce it (l. 2). She ridicules professionals dealing with quinoa, writing "Dieticians clucked over quinoa approvingly" (ll. 3/4), creating an image of scientists as hens – animals regarded as not being very bright – who are excited that the grain "tick[s] the low-fat box" (l. 4). While making fun of scientists responsible for the quinoa hype, Blythman is precise as concerns the actual nutritional facts around the grain, when she gives the reader information like the percentage of the protein content (cf. l. 8). At the same time, she again ridicules the nutritional benefits when she personifies "all those pesky […] amino acids" (l. 9), indirectly stating that these ingredients are – in a way – annoying because they are difficult for vegetarians to get enough of in their diet. Blythman frequently makes use of personifications, for example when she writes about asparagus being a "thirsty export vegetable" (l. 29) that helps to satisfy the "appetite of countries" (l. 17). This description makes asparagus seem like a human being that has certain needs that must be met whereas having an "appetite" is not vital to survival. These personifications shed a light on another strategy Blythman uses: figurative speech. She talks about "fat cat exporters and supermarkets cream[ing] off the profits" (ll. 31/32) or "a rummage through the shopping baskets" (l. 44), thereby creating vivid images in the reader's mind. Using receiver-including pronouns in phrases like "[we] struggled" (l. 2) or "countries such as ours" (l. 17) ensures that the reader does not feel personally attacked by Blythman, as she makes clear that she is part of the problem.

Blythman's use of language/register is another strategy to show the problems created by the skyrocketing consumption of quinoa. As she writes about food, she uses a wide range of terms when referring to different kinds of "eaters", such as "vegans" (title), "[a]dventurous eaters" (l. 6), "vegetarians" (l. 10), "meat avoider[s]" (l. 12), "well-intentioned … consumers" (l. 24) and "omnivores" (l. 43). Some of these terms go hand in hand with Blythman's preference for irony when she calls vegetarians and vegans "meat avoiders", a term she uses to make them appear somewhat strange. The term "omnivores" is a technical term which is mostly used in connection to wildlife, but which – technically correct – is also used with regard to human beings. Although Blythman uses technical terms (e. g. "deforestation", l. 37) her text is written in a clear and vivid style (e. g. "a rummage through the shopping baskets", l. 44).

Summing up, one can say that structure, use of rhetorical devices and register make Blythman's article varied and interesting to read. Nevertheless, one cannot fail to remark that Blythman remains vague as to where she draws her knowledge from, quoting "government healthy eating advice" to "base your meals on starchy foods"

(l. 5) without giving a source, or mentioning the nutritional benefit of quinoa and giving percentages without any reference. What is more, it must be said that Blythman gives a very one-sided view of the topic, mocking vegetarians/vegans and ridiculing the western attitude that has all the best intentions, but harms others. All in all, Blythman's article therefore has to be seen in a critical light. *(948 words)*

3. a) ***Hinweis:*** *In this task, you have to write a discussion between four different people who represent different opinions. First of all, take notes on which positions the people stand for and why (= their arguments). You can also introduce a host. Make sure that the statements fit the role and that the participants refer to each other. The task does not explicitly tell you to find a solution to the problem of globalised food production, but this could be a possible ending to the discussion. The following solution is an example:*
   - *Carla, vegan from Britain*
     - *needs quinoa for a healthy and balanced diet*
     - *is willing to pay high prices for her health*
     - *is shocked by consequences of quinoa consumption, thinks about buying substitutes*
   - *Maria, Bolivian mother of five*
     - *not able to feed her children on a healthy diet anymore*
     - *children becoming obese (fast food)*
     - *prices have soared*
     - *not only quinoa, but all kinds of vegetable have become more expensive*
   - *Antonio, Peruvian asparagus worker*
     - *suffers under the bad working conditions*
     - *earns very little money, but prices for staple food have risen dramatically*
     - *water shortages*
     - *still lucky to have a job at all*
   - *John, boss of food company*
     - *reference to supply and demand*
     - *sees problems, but does not feel responsible*
     - *responsibility for success of company*

Host: Ladies and gentlemen, in the supermarket we can buy all kinds of fruits and vegetables that we have sometimes never even heard of, such as longan and durian. "Old friends" in our cuisine like asparagus can now be purchased all year long. And now there is quinoa – the "miracle grain" from the Andes. But where do all these products come from? What about the producing countries? We are here today to discuss the consequences of globalised food production. I would like my four guests to introduce themselves and their views on this topic.

Carla: My name is Carla and I'm a vegan from Britain. In order to eat a healthy diet, I need quinoa, for example. It has so many nutritional benefits that help me make sure that I get all the vitamins and nutrients that I need. I'm so happy you can get quinoa everywhere now and not only in specialised shops. It's quite expensive, of course, but I'm willing to pay any price for my health.

Maria: But that's where the real problem starts. I'm Maria; I have five hungry mouths to feed. I'm from Bolivia, the country where quinoa has been a staple food for centuries. As quinoa has become the "superfood from the Andes" and is exported to many western countries, the price for it has more than tripled in Bolivia.

Carla: Oh, I didn't know that …

Maria: Yes, quinoa used to be the staple food of the poor people, and now it is only for the rich! Even chicken is now cheaper than quinoa. I have to feed my children with fast food now. I'm afraid they're soon going to be overweight.

Antonio: We have the same problems in Peru. My name is Antonio and I work on the asparagus fields. It is very hard labour under bad conditions, and we only get very little money. And that is not enough to buy good food for our families. Everything has become very, very expensive. And what is worse, now we have severe water problems because asparagus needs lots of water and there is not enough water where I live. So we have to pay a lot for it. Imagine – for water!! Just so that YOU can eat asparagus all year long.

John: Well, I don't think it's that simple. I'm John, by the way. I'm the boss of an international food company. First of all, Antonio, you have to recognise that at least you have a job. Before we came to your country there were hardly any jobs for farm workers. We have created thousands of new jobs. Yes, they are not that well paid, but we offer qualification courses and other benefits.

Antonio: That's right, but the problems created by globalised food production are not solved by qualifying some workers. You have to pay higher wages so that we can all live a better life!

John: If we pay higher wages, the prices for the products will go up …

Carla: That would mean we'd have to pay even more? Quinoa already costs more than £ 3 for 200 grammes!!

Maria: But you just said that you would pay any price!! The producing countries should not suffer under the consequences of globalised food production. If nobody bought quinoa anymore, the price would surely fall.

John: That's right, but then many farmers would lose their income …

Antonio: Yeah, I can understand that. But why can't we *all* profit from global food production? The consumers who get what they want for reasonable prices, the workers who get decent pay and the Bolivians and Peruvians who can still afford good food for their children? If companies gave up just part of their profit, everybody could benefit.

John: Sounds like a great idea, but we are responsible to our shareholders, of course, we have to pay wages and salaries for the people who work for us, we have to pay for transport, do the advertising, develop new products. It's not that simple.

Host: We can see that this is a very complex matter for which we won't find a solution here today. I would now like every participant to give a brief conclusion.

Carla: Well, I'll definitely check where my food comes from and do research on possible local alternatives. I believe a good balance between home-grown and imported food is important, but I still have to make sure that I can live on a healthy diet!

Maria: I hope and pray that the price for quinoa goes down again. I want my children to be able to eat good food to grow up healthily, but I don't think anything will change.

Antonio: I also believe that we in the producing country are the losers when it comes to globalised food production. We labour for little pay and the bosses make the money.

John: I can only promise that I will contact our partners in Peru and see what we can do to improve your working conditions.

Host: Thanks to all of you for the lively discussion. *(842 words)*

b) ***Hinweis:** In this task, you have to comment on a statement by Peta. Work on the following steps and take notes.*
1. Analyse the quotation.
2. Find out what it means and which view becomes obvious.
3. Determine your own position.
4. Refer to aspects dealt with in the article and/or video
Now write your comment. Start with an introduction, followed by the main part and a conclusion.
- *Analysis of statement: Parallelism and anaphora: "Eating quinoa ... but eating meat ..."; antithesis: "Bolivian farmers" vs. "us all", (contrast: "they" – "us")*
- *Meaning: The suffering of a certain group of people can be tolerated for the greater good of many.*
- *Your own opinion: either agreement or disagreement*
- *Respective information from the text and/or video*

Peta *(People for the ethical treatment of animals)* have commented on the problems Bolivian farmers are facing due to the increased quinoa consumption by vegetarians and vegans in western countries, saying that "Eating quinoa may harm Bolivian farmers, but eating meat harms us all". In the following, I am going to analyse the statement and its meaning. After that I am going to comment on Peta's stance.
The statement is structured in the form of an anaphora/parallelism: "Eating quinoa ... but eating meat ..." The second part of the anaphora is introduced by the conjunction "but", indicating opposition, which becomes obvious in the contrast between "Bolivian farmers" and "all of us". The meaning this statement conveys is that the suffering of a certain group of people can be tolerated for the greater good of many.
I cannot agree with the message imparted by this statement. From my point of view, it is unacceptable for the hardship of a group of people to just be dismissed

as not being so important. Since the nutritional benefits of quinoa for vegans and vegetarians, in particular, were advocated in western countries, the demand for this grain has increased dramatically. This has caused prices to skyrocket. Many Bolivians, for whom quinoa has been the traditional staple food, now have to face the consequences of this rise in prices: chicken is now cheaper than quinoa, and unhealthy fast food is replacing the traditional, healthy diet. This development cannot only be observed in Bolivia, but also in other countries which have focused on exporting fruit and vegetables cultivated in monocultures to western countries. Examples can also be found in Peru (asparagus) and other parts of South America (soya and cattle production). Of course, one must not forget that the producing countries profit from the export of quinoa and asparagus to a certain degree: new jobs are created, and foreign money comes into the country that could be used to improve infrastructure, education and health services, for example. However, as producers of raw products earn the least amount of money from their products, it is multinational corporations that profit most.

Considering these aspects and bearing in mind that Peta – an organisation which promotes vegetarianism and veganism as a means to save and protect animals – issued this statement, I cannot but strongly oppose the attitude conveyed. Even if one bears in mind that this statement is very pointed, one cannot fail to notice that Peta seems to believe that animals are more important than Bolivian farmers – that animals are more important than people. Of course, I am also of the opinion that animals must not suffer and need to be protected, but people's wellbeing should not be ignored either. *(452 words)*

Klausur 9: The Individual and Society/Multicultural Society

Textaufgabe 90 min.

Text: Andy Carrington, "The Fight For Love"

Pricks point and snarl
as we walk on by,
white and brown,
hand in hand,
attempting to go
where we please.

Freedom? Pah, it's a myth.

Every corner there's a man
in builders clothing
or a three-piece suit

Muttering to himself
like we're some form
of foreign disease.

"We should each stick
to our own; this country's
in even trouble as it is."

Yeah, I hear ya, moron,

I betrayed my race

And now the BNP
doesn't like either of us.

The Daily Mail's on it, too,
saying the white population
will decline rapidly
if we keep this up.

Fuck 'em.

We're British born

and bred;

No, in fact,
we're like Vice Versas
– about to make interracial
babies JUST BECAUSE
WE CAN.

Many friends have said
that I must have the soul
of a black or Indian
just 'cause I'm willing
to mix,

And most will think
of me as insane
when I say I could never
see the good in the dizzy
blondes or gothic bitches
of this world.

But ever since around
the age of twenty
I've had a thing for chocolate
women … I won't deny,

And the more I begin
to piece together my heart
and feel less and less
accepted in this country,

The more I begin
to understand the words
you once said, in faith,
as I spent one
of my nights alone,
wondering if we were ever
gonna be:

"The division of colour,
the division of class,
they're all false;

The only real and true thing
here … is love."

And I'm not ashamed
now to say that I think
you may be right. *(271 words)*

Annotations

l. 1	prick	a very offensive word for a stupid, unpleasant man
l. 10	three-piece suit	formal dress often worn by businessmen *(Anzug mit Weste)*
l. 11	to mutter	to speak in a low voice, especially when you are annoyed about something
l. 17	moron	idiot
l. 19	BNP	British National Party, a far-right political party in the United Kingdom
l. 41	dizzy	here: stupid

Material: Cartoon

© Ed Fischer/cartoonstock.com

Tasks

1. Describe the situation the speaker of the poem finds himself in and explain why he says: "Freedom? Pah, it's a myth". *(10)*
2. Analyse the speaker's reaction to this situation. *(20)*
3. Interpret the cartoon and compare its message with the message of Andy Carrington's poem. *(30)*

Hörverstehen 45 min.

Track 3

Hidden Figures author Margot Lee Shetterly

Before listening, read the tasks and look up words you need.
Listen to the interview twice.
Note that the options give the meaning but not necessarily the original wording. *(40)*

Vocabulary from the listening text
computer: here: also refers to a person who makes calculations
pivotal: *zentral*
trajectory: *Flugbahn*

1. Tick (✓) the correct box or boxes. *(9)*

   a) Margot Lee Shetterly worked on the Apollo programme.
   - ☐ true
   - ☐ false

   b) *Hidden Figures* is a book about women …
   - ☐ who had ordinary jobs.
   - ☐ who were put into space.
   - ☐ of whom many were African-American.
   - ☐ who work behind the scenes in the Air and Space Museum.
   - ☐ who worked as engineers and mathematicians.

   c) The programme “American café” is broadcast from …
   - ☐ Hampton, Virginia.
   - ☐ Washington.
   - ☐ outside the US.

2. Fill in the gap with the correct date. *(1)*

   John Glenn flew around the world on ______________________________.

3. Tick (✓) the correct box. *(4)*
   Afterwards, Glenn went on to a career as a …
   - ☐ pilot.
   - ☐ mathematician.
   - ☐ politician.
   - ☐ civil rights activist.

4. Fill in the gaps. *(3)*

"Margot Lee Shetterly tells the story of several women who played pivotal roles in ______________________. The book, which was made into an Oscar-nominated movie of the same name, tells how the female computers, many of them African Americans in the segregated South, overcame not only ____________________ bias, but also ________________ to change American society."

5. Tick (✓) the boxes with the areas that are mentioned explicitly as being the subject of segregation under the Jim Crow laws. *(5)*

- ☐ bathrooms
- ☐ courtrooms
- ☐ factories
- ☐ restaurants
- ☐ education

6. Match the following (parts of) sentences by filling in A, B and C in the right places. There are two parts more than you need. *(3)*

A. The book takes readers from the middle of World War II to

B. Katherine Johnson and her fellow computers checked

C. If Johnson said it was OK,

- ☐ the trajectories and the flight paths for space flights.
- ☐ Glenn said he was ready to go.
- ☐ Glenn's capacities and limitations as an astronaut.
- ☐ the launch of Sputnik and the Apollo programme.
- ☐ the launch of Sputnik and the beginning of the space race.

7. Tick (✓) the correct box or boxes. *(15)*

a) Margot Lee Shetterly says that "we trust our computers, …

- ☐ our phones,
- ☐ our washing machines,
- ☐ our toasters,
- ☐ our cars,
- ☐ our tablets,

everything."

b) In the early days of computers …

☐ they did not need any electrical power.
☐ they did not always give the correct answer.
☐ they sometimes stopped in the middle of a calculation.
☐ they were trusted by everyone.

c) Margot Lee Shetterly does not think that history is only made by presidents and kings and famous people and politicians.

☐ true ☐ false

d) The women described in the book did not dedicate their lives to their extraordinary jobs alone.

☐ true ☐ false

e) The women only had this one job and then had to go back and stay at home for the rest of their lives.

☐ true ☐ false

f) Margot Lee Shetterly hopes that, when learning about the "Hidden Figures", …

☐ children will learn to see NASA critically.
☐ children will want to become scientists or engineers too.

g) Margot Lee Shetterly is sceptical of the internet and cannot be found online.

☐ true ☐ false

Lösungsvorschläge

Textaufgabe

1. ***Hinweis:*** *The task consists of a description and an explanation. Your description of the situation should include the central fact that the speaker is the male part in a mixed-race couple, and you should sum up the examples he mentions of how people around the couple react to that fact. This description leads to the conclusion that they do not feel accepted in their country, which is Great Britain. This conclusion explains why the speaker thinks freedom is a myth: they cannot show their love without being discriminated against.*

   The speaker of the poem describes how people react to the fact that he, as a "white" man, is in love with a "brown" (l. 3) woman. The couple is confronted with rejection and even outright hatred. When he walks hand in hand with his partner, people on the street, who the speaker describes as "pricks" (l. 1), point at them, uttering their disgust at the mixed couple that, in their eyes, is "some form of foreign disease" (ll. 12/13). The couple experience this kind of rejection from people of the working class ("builders clothing", l. 9) as well as from businessmen ("three-piece suit", l. 10). In the eyes of these people, the speaker has "betrayed [his] race" (l. 18). The British National Party (BNP) and tabloid newspapers like the Daily Mail make similar racist comments, describing mixed relationships as a threat to the white population (cf. ll. 19–24). Even the speaker's friends seem unwilling to simply accept their love, wondering whether he has "the soul of a black or Indian" (ll. 34/35) and thinking of him as "insane" (l. 38) As a result, he feels "less and less accepted in this country" (ll. 50/51), which is Great Britain. He and his partner cannot show their love openly without receiving hostile remarks, and thus, for him, the supposed freedom in British society is only a myth. *(228 words)*

2. ***Hinweis:*** *As you are asked here to analyse the speaker's reaction, you should again describe what he says and explain what kind of feelings he expresses and what effect the situation has on the couple: they show defiance and are united in their resistance against the hatred they are confronted with. It makes sense to quote passages from the text to substantiate your analysis.*

   As the title of the poem "The Fight For Love" indicates, the couple is unwilling to back down. They defy the rejection they experience ("Fuck 'em", l. 25), insisting on the fact that they are as "British" as the people who harass them (cf. ll. 26/27). Their defiant pose against the accusation of bringing down the "white race" is highlighted in their announcement that they are "about to make interracial babies JUST BECAUSE WE CAN" (ll. 30–32), the only part of the poem in capital letters. In fact, the hostility of their environment brings them even closer together. The speaker remembers one moment when he was alone and doubting whether their relationship would be strong enough. In this situation, his partner told him that the divisions of colour and class were all wrong, and the only true thing was love (cf. ll. 59–63). In the final lines of the poem, the speaker addresses his partner, telling her that she "may be right" (ll. 65/66) in saying so. Even though the "may" sounds tentative, it expresses the hope that their love will overcome all the obstacles that society puts in front of them. *(195 words)*

3. ***Hinweis:*** *An interpretation of a cartoon starts with a description of what can be seen in the picture. In this case, you also have to explain why the policeman apologises to the white driver of the car and what his remark "I thought you were black" tells the reader about his attitude towards black people. The caption provides the context of the scene and refers to Martin Luther King Day, the holiday which honours the most important spokesman for racial equality and civil rights. The cartoon points out the gap between the "talk of progress" in American society and the attitude of people like the policeman, who are still full of racial prejudice. Comparing the cartoon and the poem, they could be said to have the same message: despite formal racial equality, there is still a lot of informal discrimination in everyday life.*

The cartoon shows a policeman who has just stopped a car. When he notices that the driver is white, the policeman apologises, saying, "Sorry, I thought you were black". The caption "Sometime, just after all the talk about progress on Martin Luther King Day", makes the message of the cartoon quite clear: even though Martin Luther King has been honoured with his own national holiday, the progress made in the fight for racial equality, which is emphasised on this day, is often refuted by reality. The policeman's apology shows that he is prejudiced against black people. In his eyes, they are to be mistrusted because they are the ones who commit crimes. The cartoon points out the discrepancy between the official talk about progress towards racial equality and the discrimination many black people still experience by whites.

Although the cartoon refers to a specific situation in America, and Carrington's poem reflects on experiences made in British society, the message of poem and cartoon is similar: freedom and equality for everyone, no matter what class or race they belong to, is still only a myth. Despite the fact that the Civil Rights Movement, of which King was the most famous spokesperson, brought about groundbreaking changes, racism is still present in many people's minds. Black people may formally have the same rights as white people, but they still experience discrimination in their everyday lives. The fact that a mixed couple has to fight for their love and to be accepted in a western society like Great Britain is only one example of widespread prejudice and hatred even though equal rights have been formally installed for everyone. *(274 words)*

Hörverstehen

Transkript: *Hidden Figures* author Margot Lee Shetterly

David Bird: Welcome to the American café. I'm your host, David Bird. March is national women's history month here in the United States. This week we talk to Margot Lee Shetterly, the author of the book *Hidden Figures* about those women, many of them African American, who helped put the United States into space and on the moon.

Margot Lee Shetterly: They had a complete life and you know what we would call kind of a normal life. They just had this extraordinary job.

David Bird: Margot Lee Shetterly and the women of *Hidden Figures* on this week's American café.

(Music)

David Bird: The Smithsonian's National Air and Space Museum sits about a block away from our headquarters building here in Washington. Walk into the main lobby and you will see the Mercury capsule 'Friendship Seven', which John Glenn flew around the earth on February 20th, 1962. Glenn was hailed as a hero, was awarded the space congressional medal of honour and went on to a career in public service including several terms as a US senator. But his flight might never have happened, had it not been for a dedicated group of engineers and mathematicians on a spit of land near Hampton, Virginia. In her book *Hidden Figures* the story of the African-American women who helped win the space race, Margot Lee Shetterly tells the story of several women who played pivotal roles in that race to space. The book, which was made into an Oscar-nominated movie of the same name, tells how the female computers, many of them African Americans in the segregated South, overcame not only race bias, but also sexism to change American society.

Margot Lee Shetterly: You know these women worked during the time of Jim Crow segregation, legalised segregation in terms of bathrooms, cafeterias, eating establishments, schools, graveyards, absolutely everything. And those issues, or those laws circumscribed what they were able to do, but it also provided, or they saw those things as things that had to be dismantled, you know, and they really had to pick their battles.

David Bird: Shetterly says women like Dorothy Vaughn, Mary Jackson, Katherine Johnson and others used the excellence of their work as mathematicians to break through racial and gender stereotypes.

Margot Lee Shetterly: One of the things that they did was in the excellence of their work through networking and finding other excellent women to do, to fill the positions that were available there at the laboratory. And to really, you know, challenge the idea of what was possible from a woman or an African American, or an African-American woman.

David Bird: Shetterly's book takes readers from the middle of World War II to the launch of Sputnik and the beginning of the space race. Katherine Johnson and her fellow computers checked the trajectories and the flight paths for space flights. They were so trusted that John Glenn said to have the girl, meaning Katherine Johnson, check the computations of his historic flight, which had been calculated by a then state of the art IBM computer. If Johnson said it was OK, Glenn said he was ready to go. Margot Lee Shetterly told me that Katherine Johnson and her colleagues made sure the flight was ready for launch.

Margot Lee Shetterly: We trust our computers and our toasters, our phones, our cars, everything. We always just sort of assume that they are correct and they're pointing us in the right direction. Well those were the early days of computers and people did not trust them, you know sometimes they did not give always the right answer. Sometimes they just stopped working in the middle of a calculation and so this human check on the machine was a really important part of that transition.

David Bird: Shetterley is herself a product of the space program, her father worked at the NASA Langley research center where much of the book takes place. One question she often gets asked is, 'why did this story take so long to come out?' Margot told me that history is often made by normal people who were just doing their jobs.

Margot Lee Shetterly: I think what it really means is we have this idea of history as something that comes from presidents and kings and famous people and politicians. When history is really what each of us does each day. You know and what these women did each day was to get up and go to work and work at NASA as professional mathematicians. You know they came home, they took care of their children and their husbands, and their homes and, you know, they were girl scout leaders and things like that, so they had a complete life and you know what we would call kind of a normal life. They just had these extraordinary jobs.

David Bird: One of the computers, Katherine Johnson, went on to work on the Apollo program and helped calculate trajectories that put astronauts Neil Armstrong and Buzz Aldrin on the moon. Others helped women advance at the space agency or help to train the next generation of female engineers and mathematicians. […]

Margot Lee Shetterly: I know how excited kids get when they're presented with the dream, you know, that comes from space travel and exploring our earth and looking beyond and, you know, all those different things so, you know, I really hope that maybe there are people out there listening and, you know, those of us who aren't officially affiliated with NASA, but really believe in that mission, that can kind of pick up the slack on that education. I think that, you know, building the next generation of scientists, engineers, mathematicians is a really important thing.

David Bird: To learn more about Margot Lee Shetterly – you can find her at her website margotleeshetterly.com. You can also find her book *Hidden Figures* at your favourite retailer or online. And the Oscar-nominated film is in theaters. […] Thanks for listening. Until next time. I'm David Bird in Washington. *(1 004 words)*

Hinweise: *zu 1 a) und b): "Margot Lee Shetterly, the author of the book* 'Hidden Figures' *about those women, many of them African American, who helped put the United States into space and on the moon". (ll. 3–5); "a dedicated group of engineers and mathematicians" (l. 17); zu 1. c): "here in Washington" (l. 12)*
zu 2: "... Mercury capsule 'Friendship Seven', which John Glenn flew around the earth on February 20th, 1962." (ll. 13/14)
zu 3: "several terms as a US senator" (l. 16)
zu 4: ll. 18–23
zu 5: ll. 24–26
zu 6: ll. 38–45
zu 7 a): ll. 46/47; zu 7 b): ll. 48–51; zu 7 c): "When history is really what each of us does each day." (l. 58); zu 7 d) und e): ll. 60–67; zu 7 f) "... pick up the slack of that education ... building the next generation of scientists ..." (ll. 68–74); zu 7 g): "To learn more about Margot Lee Shetterly – you can find her at her website margotlee-shetterly.com.*" (ll. 75/76)*

1. a) Margot Lee Shetterly worked on the Apollo programme.
   - ☐ true
   - ☑ false

   b) *Hidden Figures* is a book about women …
   - ☐ who had ordinary jobs.
   - ☐ who were put into space.
   - ☑ of whom many were African-American.
   - ☐ who work behind the scenes in the Air and Space Museum.
   - ☑ who worked as engineers and mathematicians.

   c) The programme "American café" is broadcast from …
   - ☐ Hampton, Virginia.
   - ☑ Washington.
   - ☐ outside the US.

2. John Glenn flew around the world on **February 20th, 1962 / 20(th) February 1962 / 20/2/1962** (BE) / **2/20/1962** (AE)

3. Afterwards, Glenn went on to a career as a …
   - ☐ pilot.
   - ☐ mathematician.
   - ☑ politician.
   - ☐ civil rights activist.

4. "Margot Lee Shetterly tells the story of several women who played pivotal roles in **the race to space**. The book, which was made into an Oscar-nominated movie of the same name, tells how the female computers, many of them African Americans in the segregated South, overcame not only **race** bias, but also **sexism** to change American society."

5. ✓ bathrooms
   ☐ courtrooms
   ☐ factories
   ✓ restaurants
   ✓ education

6. Match the following (parts of) sentences by filling in A, B and C in the right places. There are two parts more than you need.

   A. The book takes readers from the middle of World War II to
   B. Katherine Johnson and her fellow computers checked
   C. If Johnson said it was OK,

   [B] the trajectories and the flight paths for space flights.
   [C] Glenn said he was ready to go.
   [ ] Glenn's capacities and limitations as an astronaut.
   [ ] the launch of Sputnik and the Apollo programme.
   [A] the launch of Sputnik and the beginning of the space race.

7. a) Margot Lee Shetterly says that "we trust our computers, …
   ✓ our phones,
   ☐ our washing machines,
   ✓ our toasters,
   ✓ our cars,
   ☐ our tablets,
   everything."

b) In the early days of computers …

- [ ] they did not need any electrical power.
- [x] they did not always give the correct answer.
- [x] they sometimes stopped in the middle of a calculation.
- [ ] they were trusted by everyone.

c) Margot Lee Shetterly does not think that history is only made by presidents and kings and famous people and politicians.

- [x] true
- [ ] false

d) The women described in the book did not dedicate their lives to their extraordinary jobs alone.

- [x] true
- [ ] false

e) The women only had this one job and then had to go back and stay at home for the rest of their lives.

- [ ] true
- [x] false

f) Margot Lee Shetterly hopes that, when learning about the "Hidden Figures",

- [ ] children will learn to see NASA critically.
- [x] children will want to become scientists or engineers too.

g) Margot Lee Shetterly is sceptical of the internet and cannot be found online.

- [ ] true
- [x] false

Klausur 10: Dystopian Fiction/Science and Technology

Textaufgabe 180 min.

Gemma Malley, *The Resistance*

Gemma Malley's dystopian novel The Resistance *is set in the UK in 2140. For some decades, people have been taking longevity drugs, prolonging their lives almost indefinitely, which has resulted in severe overpopulation. In order to reduce population figures and manage the resources available, people are no longer allowed to have children. Children born despite this are labelled "Surplus" and taken to facilities where they are trained to be "Valuable Assets", i. e. servants to the adults; some Surpluses are also taken to research facilities for other purposes.*

Hillary shot an uncomfortable look in the girls' direction, then looked away quickly. 'These are Surpluses? Why are they here?'

'My question, Hillary. Answer my question, please.'

Hillary sighed. 'They have their uses, some of them. But yes, overall, they are a drain. Richard, why am I here? I want to see the drugs, not these girls.'

'You are here because the Authorities must sanction the means as well as the end,' Richard said smoothly. 'Sanction and protect our production lines from prying eyes, from questions, from people who don't understand science, who don't realise that every move forward in science requires a … a freedom not afforded all disciplines.'

'Freedom? What do you mean?' Hillary asked.

'What if I was to tell you that Surpluses were the key to the health and wellbeing of mankind?' Richard said. 'What if I was to tell you that Surpluses are not a burden, but our saviours? That they are, in fact, not Surpluses at all, but Valuable Assets?' […]

[He] gestured towards the row of beds.

'Think of them as incubators. Incubators that can grow state-of-the-art embryonic stem cells,' he said reverently.

'Embryonic? You mean …'

'I mean, embryos. Ten at a time. We're hoping to get up to twelve today. […].'

'And you're making them? Here?' Hillary gasped.

'It's not that radical, Hillary. Remember IVF, or was that before your time? You take an egg, you fertilise it, you put it in the womb. Only we do four, five, ten, twenty. We let them take hold, let them grow, then we harvest them – and the cells, Hillary, the cells can do anything. Take a precursor stem cell and subject it to the Longevity formula, and the results are … well, they're beautiful. Astounding. Revolutionary. Two weeks is all it takes, Hillary. Two weeks from fertilisation.'

Hillary looked up at him in wonderment.

'But the supply,' she said, her forehead wrinkled in concentration. 'The supply's not high enough. Not to supply the country, let alone the world. There aren't enough Surpluses. It's not sustainable.'

[Richard] laughed. 'Of course it's sustainable. We just have to make sure we control the supply.'

'But how? There's no guarantee …'

'No guarantee?' [He] smiled, shook his head. Then he lowered his voice. 'You and the Authorities know full well that Surpluses have been used for new ingredients for years – blood donation, bone marrow, stem cells. We've always needed a certain level of supply of Surpluses for medical research, and certain departments within the Authorities have been most … sympathetic. But until now, it's been low level – a few faulty birth-control implants here and there ensured an adequate supply. All I'm saying now is that we need to crank it up. We need more young flesh, more Valuable Assets. Officially.'

[…]

'The Authorities … you mean, we sanctioned the creation of Surpluses?' Hillary's mouth was open in shock.

'You didn't know?' [He] asked, his tone surprised. 'I thought you'd read Adrian's notes. He gave us special dispensation. And now we need to plant more. We need large numbers. Surplus farms. They are our lifeblood, Hillary. The potential is unending.'

[…]

'There are channels, Richard. You'd be breaking protocols and regulations …'

'Protocols and regulations that will be swept aside when people understand what the drugs can do. Protocols and regulations that are outdated, that belong to another time. This is progress. This is the future.'

Hillary was silent for a few moments, then she looked back at the row of beds.

'This girl here,' she said, pointing to the girl clamped to the bed. 'What's happening to her?'

'Ah, well, she's at the most exciting stage of the process. Our first twelve, I believe. Twelve embryos, about two weeks old, are being extracted. Twelve embryos with enough stem cells to provide London and the Home Counties with Longevity+ for three months.'

'You mean she's pregnant?'

'Pregnant as a sow,' he confirmed. […]

'And what will happen to her … afterwards?'

'Afterwards?' Richard looked at her uncertainly.

'Will she blab? We can't have the girls talking.' […]

'Oh, I see,' Richard said, looking relieved. 'No, she won't be able to blab. To start with, each girl has a good fifteen years of production ahead of her, I'd say. After that, who knows.'

'Who knows? […] What will happen to the girls when they are no longer Valuable? We can't keep creating Surpluses if they're going to become Burdens later on.'

'Burdens? Oh, they won't be Burdens,' Richard said, smiling lightly. 'They'll just become Valuable in other ways. […] There are many wonderful things to be harvested from the human body, Hillary. The possibilities are endless.'

'It's incredible,' Hillary breathed. 'Who'd have thought Surpluses could be so useful?' *(789 words)*

Gemma Malley: The Resistance. London: Bloomsbury 2008, pp. 424–247

Tasks

1. Outline the use of Surpluses in Richard's research facility. *(10)*
2. Examine Richard's attitude towards his research, the Authorities and the Surpluses, taking into account his use of language. *(20)*
3. You are a Surplus who has joined a resistance movement opposing Longevity. Write a leaflet to make people aware of the Surpluses' situation and make them join the fight against Longevity drugs. *(30)*

Sprachmittlung 60 min.

Suche nach den Genen für ein langes Leben – Muntere Methusaleme

Altern? Polypen kennen das Problem nicht. Nun weisen sie Forschern den Weg zum Quell der ewigen Regeneration. von Adelheid Müller-Lissner

Herakles war um diese Aufgabe nicht zu beneiden: Wie sollte er die Hydra besiegen, das Wesen mit den vielen Köpfen, dem auf der Stelle zwei davon nachwuchsen, wenn ihr einer abgeschlagen wurde? Zumal das garstige Tier in der Mitte ohnehin einen unsterblichen Kopf trug?

Auch einem kaum einen Zentimeter langen, filigranen Süßwasserpolypen haben Biologen den Namen Hydra gegeben. Unsterblich ist der vergleichsweise einfache Organismus zwar nicht, doch seit Jahren fasziniert er Forscher, die sich dem menschlichen Sehnsuchtsthema Langlebigkeit widmen. Denn Hydras haben eine beneidenswerte Regenerationskraft: Nimmermüde Stammzellen mit konstanter Teilungsrate ermöglichen es ihnen nicht nur, verletzte oder zerstörte Körperteile nachzubauen. Sie können auch binnen weniger Wochen alle Zellen ihres Körpers komplett erneuern. Gute Voraussetzungen, um den Prozessen des Alterns und Sterbens zu entkommen. Aber kann sie Hydra wirklich nutzen?

[…]

Am Max-Planck-Institut für demografische Forschung in Rostock wurde im Jahr 2006 ein einzigartiges Langzeitexperiment gestartet […]. [Die] Mitarbeiter des Rostocker Instituts [versorgen] tagaus tagein an die 1 800 der winzigen Tierchen, die sie einzeln in Glasgefäßen halten. Pro Untersuchungsjahr starben dabei im Durchschnitt nur fünf – und das meistens nicht an „Altersschwäche", sondern durch Unfälle in den Glasbehältern, in denen sie einzeln und vor Feinden geschützt leben. Fünf Prozent eines Jahrgangs könnten auf diese Art ihren 500. Geburtstag erreichen, meinen die Forscher. In zwei der fünf Kohorten bestehe sogar die Chance, dass jeder Zwanzigste 3 000 Jahre alt werde. Zudem gibt es keine Anzeichen dafür, dass die Fruchtbarkeit der Winzlinge mit den Jahren abnimmt. […]

[…]

Zugleich nahm das Sterberisiko mit zunehmendem Lebensalter nicht zu – im Unterschied zum Menschen, bei dem sich das Risiko, im nächsten Jahr zu sterben, ab dem Alter von 35 Jahren alle acht Jahre verdoppelt und am 80. Geburtstag bei eins zu zehn liegt. […] Gebrechlichkeit, körperlicher und geistiger Abbau, sie schienen bisher unausweichlich. […]

Als nützlich könnten sich die Süßwasserpolypen auch im Kampf gegen eine Krankheit erweisen, die viele Menschen vor Erreichen eines „gesegneten Alters“ dahinrafft: Krebs. „Die Krebszelle teilt sich schließlich wie die Zellen der Hydra unaufhörlich,“ sagt [Ralf] Schaible, [Mitautor der Studie]. An den Polypen könnte man deshalb studieren, wie Zellen sich davon abbringen lassen.

[…]

Wenn nicht alle mehrzelligen, fortpflanzungsfähigen Lebewesen altern, stellen sich aber auch die alten Grundsatzfragen neu: Was bedeutet Altern? Warum altern die allermeisten Lebewesen? Und: Kann man das nicht auch bei komplexen Organismen wie dem Menschen verhindern? Aufschlüsse über die letzte Frage erhoffen sich Forscher allerdings eher von Organismen, die nicht alt werden. Etwa vom Türkisen Prachtgrundkärpfling, einem kleinen Fisch aus Südostafrika, der rasant wächst, früh geschlechtsreif wird, im Zeitraffer altert – und dessen Lebensspanne meist nur eine Regenzeit umfasst. Am Leibniz-Institut für Alternsforschung in Jena haben Matthias Platzer und seine Kollegen im Jahr 2013 das Genom des Fischs mit dem zoologischen Namen *Nothobranchius furzeri* entschlüsselt. Nun versuchen sie, gezielt Gene des Fischs auszuschalten oder zu aktivieren, um herauszufinden, wo im Genom die Regionen für das Altern liegen. […]

Ob man sein kurzes Dasein dennoch „glücklich“ nennen kann, wird sich wohl für immer der Kenntnis von Wissenschaftlern entziehen. Für Menschen sind Glücksgefühle, wenn es um die Frage nach dem guten Leben geht, aber womöglich ein wichtigeres Kriterium als seine schiere Länge. Zudem haben Studien Hinweise dafür geliefert, dass beides zusammenhängt, dass also optimistische Lebenseinstellung und großes subjektives Wohlbefinden sich letztlich auch auf die Lebenserwartung auswirken.

[…]

Wer hat, dem wird gegeben? Wer schon das Glück hat, glücklich zu sein, dem wird auch noch ein langes Leben geschenkt? Dieser These widerspricht jetzt eine in „Lancet“ erschienene Langzeituntersuchung von über 700 000 Frauen aus der britischen Million Women Study: Die Selbsteinstufung als „glücklich“ hatte bei ihnen keine direkten Auswirkungen auf die Wahrscheinlichkeit, in zehn Jahren noch zu leben.

Einen indirekten Zusammenhang gibt es aber trotzdem, denn viele Frauen, die zum Zeitpunkt der Befragung krank waren, fühlten sich deshalb auch psychisch schlechter, und sie lebten mit größerer Wahrscheinlichkeit zehn Jahre später nicht mehr. Betrachteten die Forscher jedoch nur die Frauen, die zu Beginn bei guter Gesundheit waren, konnten sie keinen „glücksbedingten“ Unterschied in der Lebenserwartung finden.

Den Winzlingen in den Rostocker Laborgefäßen geben die Forscher sicherheitshalber seit Jahren alles, was sie zu ihrem Glück brauchen – um ihre Chancen auf ein extrem langes Leben zu maximieren. Ihre Ansprüche sind ja auch vergleichsweise bescheiden: Wasser mit Mineralstoffen und konstanter Temperatur, Sicherheit vor Feinden, die ihnen ans Leben wollen. Und jeden Tag kleine Krebse, ihre Lieblingsspeise.

(743 words)

Task

You are taking part in an international school project on longevity. You are researching current developments in science.
Write a blog entry for the project blog "Living Forever – just a dream?" in which you sum up relevant information from the article above. *(30)*

Lösungsvorschläge

Textaufgabe

1. ***Hinweis:*** *In this task you are asked to focus on only one aspect of the excerpt: the use of Surpluses. Scan the text for relevant information and highlight it, then make sure you sketch the main points briefly in your own words. Two aspects need to be mentioned:*
   - *medical research*
   - *production of embryos which are used to create the longevity drug*

   The instruction "outline" requires you to be neutral and not state your opinion, even though you might be tempted to comment on this inhumane way of treating people.

   In the excerpt taken from Gemma Malley's *The Resistance*, Surpluses are used in two different ways. First of all, their body matter – blood and bone marrow, for example – is used for medical research. Second, Surpluses are used to create embryos. This is done by fertilising a girl's egg, putting it in the womb and then using a procedure which is not described in detail, but which results in the growth of multiple embryos (as many as twelve) at the same time. After two weeks, the embryos are extracted and their stem cells are used to create a drug called Longevity+. Surpluses can be used like this for about fifteen years. After that, their body matter can be used in other ways, as outlined above. *(124 words)*

2. ***Hinweis:*** *In this task you are to give a thorough analysis of a character's attitude towards three different aspects. The fact that you are to take into account Richard's use of language tells you that this task is about the way he indirectly characterises himself. You may want to deal with each aspect separately first, since you have to reread the text closely. While reading, highlight evidence of Richard's attitude and note down your observations on his use of language and rhetorical devices. You will find that the aspects you are focusing on give you a coherent picture of this character. Your answer should include the following points:*
   - *Richard is a passionate scientist*
   - *he feels that he is above the law because of his achievements*
   - *he is ruthless and inhumane*

   After a short introductory sentence, present your findings. Make sure you give a statement on his attitude towards each aspect, using textual evidence, and elaborate on it. Finish the text with a concluding sentence.

   Richard is an avid scientist who is excited about his work. When talking about the girls being used as human incubators, his tone is reverent (ll. 15/16) and he uses the adjective "state-of-the-art" in connection with an anadiplosis/repetition ("… incubators. Incubators that can grow state-of-the art embryonic stem cells …"), which shows that he is proud of his invention and wants Hillary to acknowledge his

achievement. The short, clipped sentences he uses in lines 20 to 25 show how involved he is with the process and point to his impatience to have the process sanctioned by the Authorities. His enthusiasm is also tangible in the hyperbole "the cells can do anything" (l. 23) and the climax "... beautiful. Astounding. Revolutionary" (l. 24). The fact that he addresses Hillary directly and uses words with a positive connotation like "beautiful", "astounding", and "revolutionary", and cites figures to convince her reveals his eagerness; the figures also show that he is only interested in the process and its output, and that he does not think of his actions as being highly immoral in the slightest. He openly shows his disregard for the Authorities by referring to their "prying eyes" (l. 7), which is a negative metonymy for someone who checks on someone else's actions, and by condescendingly calling them "people who don't understand science" and considers his research above the law, which is clear from his claim that "every move forward in science requires a [...] freedom not afforded all disciplines" (ll. 7–9) Although he is convinced that his actions are justified by the end they serve – prolonging life – there is a slight pause before the euphemistic remark "a freedom not afforded all disciplines". From this the reader can tell that he is aware of his actions not being legal, and that he is trying to sweeten the pill for Hillary. While his hesitation might point to a bad conscience or insecurity about Hillary's reaction, lines 49–51 leave no doubt: he uses anaphora and parallelisms in a short speech to overcome Hillary's qualms and clearly state his belief that he is above the Authorities because of the progress he has made.
Richard's attitude towards the Surpluses corresponds to the fact that he is a scientist first and foremost: he shows no regard for the fact that they are humans. This is clear from his choice of words as he talks about a "supply" (l. 36) of Surpluses, "harvest[ing]" (l. 22) the stem cells and the "sustainab[ility]" (l. 30) of using Surpluses. These phrases are usually used to talk about economic issues or crops. He also refers to the Surpluses as "young flesh" (l. 39) and "incubators" (l. 15), thus turning them into mere objects. Even when Richard uses phrases with a positive connotation to refer to Surpluses, such as "valuable", "wonderful" and "the possibilities are endless", he only uses them to outline the use of their bodies in research and medicine. In other words, to him, Surpluses are like laboratory animals.
All in all, Richard is enthusiastic about his research and he has no moral scruples, which is shown by his very inhumane attitude towards Surpluses. He also ignores the regulations set by the Authorities. *(534 words)*

3. ***Hinweis:*** *This creative task tests your use of language to convince your readership. As your readership is unaware of the Surplus situation, and since they are on Longevity drugs themselves, you will have to write a convincing text to support your cause. To add emphasis to your text, use stylistic devices, such as anaphora or anadiplosis (repetition). You should also take the following aspects into account:*
   - *catchy or provoking introduction: something is wrong in the world and you are one of the people suffering because of it*
   - *longevity is unnatural*
   - *suffering: longevity drugs are produced under inhumane conditions, Surpluses*

are used to produce the ingredients
- *injustice: people who take longevity drugs rob the next generation of their lives as free and independent individuals, enslavement of children*
- *appeal to your readership and solution: name the things they can do to help*

Something is wrong in our world!

A drain on resources, an invaluable being, a Surplus: some time ago the Authorities decided that my life was worth nothing. Yet here I am, writing this and reaching out to you.

The source of eternal life
Look at yourselves and the lives you lead: you have drugs to boost your bodies' regenerative abilities, you have been given the one thing humanity has been striving for since time began – eternal life.
But did you ever pause to think that this gift comes at a cost? There is a high price to pay, and it is not measured in pounds or gold, it is measured in human lives. Longevity drugs, as you all know, feature stem cells. Stem cells grown in laboratories. Laboratories run and monitored by the Authorities. Yet do you know how stem cells are actually grown? If you paid attention in biology class, you would know that the most potent stem cells can be taken from human embryos – yes, embryos, unborn children. How is that even possible in a world where children are no longer born? The answer is: Surpluses.

Crops to be harvested
While everybody believes that we are useless, it is actually we who provide you with your drugs. There are hundreds of us: female Surpluses kept in research facilities, fertilised like cattle, used as human incubators for the embryos which are then harvested and used to make your drugs – the same way you might harvest tomatoes or carrots and turn them into sauce. While these vegetables have no sense of pain or memory, we suffer for years and years, constantly impregnated and "harvested" until our bodies are exhausted and put to other uses – we become lab rats, involuntary organ donors or endure other unimaginable cruelties. Our blood is on the hands of each and every person who takes Longevity drugs. Users of Longevity drugs are not just living on borrowed time but on time stolen from another human being in the cruellest way imaginable. How can anyone live in peace knowing this?

Upsetting Mother Nature
Let's face the facts: every time a person takes longevity drugs, dozens of children are condemned to the life of a slave, contravening the order of nature. Some time ago there used to be a balance: parents took care of their children until they reached adulthood and the children took care of their aging parents in return. But not any more. Adults used to look after and protect the young and helpless so that they could live and thrive. But not any more. There were Authorities which promoted the rights of children. But not any more. The very act of taking longevity drugs is a hubris against the highest authority: nature itself. How can anyone live for decades, having this on their conscience?

If you believe, as I do, that it is wrong to deprive children of their right to live, their right to have a full life and their freedom to choose their own path in life, join us, spread the word and fight for the justice of future generations! Let's restore the balance and order that is right because nature gave it to us – and stop taking Longevity drugs! *(537 words)*

Sprachmittlung

Hinweis: *To tackle this task successfully, first think of your target group and the purpose of your text. This will help you choose the relevant information and the register you use. Since you are writing a blog entry, your text will need to be logically structured and include a thought-provoking introduction and a catchy conclusion. You do not need to come up with a title of your own. The title already gives you a hint that will help you choose the relevant information for your text. This text is for a school project, so you need to use at least a semi-formal register as it might also be read by people other than those in your project.*
Information you need to include:
- *hydra: what it is, what it can do, what scientists hope to achieve*
- *Nothobranchius furzeri: what it is, what it can do, what scientists hope to achieve*
- *findings on human longevity*

Living forever – just a dream?

Longevity – living to be as old as Methuselah while retaining your mental and physical capacities – has been on the minds of many scientists for a long time. Now it seems as if they are one step closer to finding out how bodies can regenerate and how life might be prolonged.
One area of research deals with a freshwater polyp, about one centimetre long, endowed with a mechanism that allows it to regenerate admirably fast, which seems to enable it to defy aging. Since its stem cells divide constantly, it can regrow parts of its body which have been destroyed, and even renew every single cell in its body within weeks. Scientists have called this species "Hydra", based on the legend of Heracles and the monster which can grow two heads after one has been cut off.
Since 2006, a long-term experiment has been carried out at the Max Plank Institute in Rostock to find out whether this species' ability to regenerate can be used to prolong life: about 1,800 of the tiny creatures are kept in single water containers at a constant temperature, fed and cared for. Every year, about five of them die – not of old age but mostly due to accidents in the glass containers. Five percent might live to be 500 and some might even live for 3,000 years. Not only does it seem as if they do not get infertile with age, unlike humans, whose mental and physical abilities deteriorate from the age of 35, hydra's risk of dying does not increase with age. The species might also prove useful in cancer research: cancer cells also divide constantly, so researching the polyps may enable scientists to find out how to prevent cells from doing that.

An entirely different branch of research at the Leibniz Institute of Gerontology in Jena focuses on a small kind of fish in southeast Africa, *Nothobranchius furzeri,* which grows rapidly and becomes sexually mature early, but ages extremely fast and only lives for one season. In 2013, scientists succeeded at decoding its genome. In order to find out which regions of the genome carry the information on aging, they are now trying to activate and deactivate single genes.

However, when looking at human longevity, there is one more factor to be considered which the scientists in Rostock and Jena will be unable to look into: happiness. Some studies show that there is a connection between an optimistic attitude towards life, an individual's subjective wellbeing and their actual life expectancy. Yet the British Million Women Study contradicts these findings: the long-term study shows that participants rating themselves as happy had no direct influence on the probability that they would still be alive in ten years. The only participants who had a greater probability of dying within the next ten years were those who were ill at the time the study was carried out and considered themselves less happy because of their illness.

In a nutshell, although there are many promising scientific approaches helping scientists to understand aging better, there is no "cure" for aging on the horizon just yet.

(521 words)

Klausur 11: Shakespeare, Macbeth

Hörverstehen 20 min.

Track 4

Fair is foul and foul is fair – Shakespeare's *Macbeth*

Neil MacGregor, Director of the British Museum from 2002–2015, uses artefacts from William Shakespeare's time for an object-based journey through British history on BBC Radio 4.

Read the tasks and items below, then listen to the recording and complete the tasks. You will listen to the recording twice. *(24)*

1. Tick (✓) the correct answer. Leith pier is the place where … *(1)*
   - ☐ English ships set off on their perilous voyages.
   - ☐ Scottish ships embarked on their journeys.
   - ☐ the Scottish met people from all parts of Europe.
   - ☐ ships were built.

2. Complete: A young Scot started his voyage in ____________________

   and came back ______________________________. *(2)*

3. Name the creatures who were made responsible for the bad weather conditions during the king's voyage. *(1)*

   ____

4. Tick (✓) the correct answer. The witches we encounter in *Macbeth* … *(1)*
   - ☐ cause a restoration of power in Scotland.
   - ☐ fight chaos on land and sea.
   - ☐ solve people's problems.
   - ☐ trigger problems in all aspects of life.

5. Name two characteristics of the ship model: *(2)*

   ____

6. Tick (✓) the correct answer. This model ship … *(1)*
   - ☐ shows evidence of Scottish inventiveness.
   - ☐ serves as a record of actual ships.
   - ☐ is a way to show a survivor's gratitude.
   - ☐ helps us to understand something about how to survive at sea.

7. Complete:
For many of Shakespeare's contemporaries, witchcraft was … *(2)*

____.

8. Tick (✓) the correct answer. The social historian Keith Thomas explains that people at that time used witchcraft to … *(1)*
   - ☐ understand the physical world.
   - ☐ effect a change.
   - ☐ grasp the supernatural.
   - ☐ recognise metaphysical workings.

9. Name two methods used by white witches to heal people. *(2)*

____

____

10. Name two things black witches could apparently do. *(2)*

____

____

11. Tick (✓) the correct answer. Because of the interest in evil spirits, many books were written about how … *(1)*
   - ☐ black masses were conducted.
   - ☐ to become a witch.
   - ☐ witches renounced their pact with God.
   - ☐ witches used their power.

12. Name a thing that happened to people who were considered witches. *(1)*

____

13. Name the difference between Scottish and English witches. *(1)*

____

14. Outline the effect of Shakespeare putting the focus on witches. *(2)*

____

15. What is the intention of the extract you have listened to?
Name two aspects. *(4)*

____

____

Textaufgabe 160 min.

Macbeth, Act III, Scene II. The palace.

[…]

Lady Macbeth: Nought's had, all's spent,
Where our desire is got without content:
'Tis safer to be that which we destroy
Than by destruction dwell in doubtful joy.

Enter Macbeth

How now, my lord! why do you keep alone,
Of sorriest fancies your companions making,
Using those thoughts which should indeed have died
With them they think on? Things without all remedy
Should be without regard: what's done is done.

Macbeth: We have scotch'd the snake, not kill'd it:
She'll close and be herself, whilst our poor malice
Remains in danger of her former tooth.
But let the frame of things disjoint, both the worlds suffer,
Ere we will eat our meal in fear, and sleep
In the affliction of these terrible dreams
That shake us nightly: better be with the dead,
Whom we, to gain our peace, have sent to peace,
Than on the torture of the mind to lie
In restless ecstasy. Duncan is in his grave;
After life's fitful fever he sleeps well;
Treason has done his worst: nor steel, nor poison,
Malice domestic, foreign levy, nothing,
Can touch him further.

Lady Macbeth: Come on:
Gentle my lord, sleek o'er your rugged looks;
Be bright and jovial among your guests to-night.

Macbeth: So shall I, Love; and so, I pray, be you:
Let your remembrance apply to Banquo:
Present him eminence, both with eye and tongue:
Unsafe the while, that we
Must lave our honours in these flattering streams,
And make our faces vizards to our hearts,
Disguising what they are.

Lady Macbeth: You must leave this.

Macbeth: O, full of scorpions is my mind, dear wife!
Thou know'st that Banquo, and his Fleance, lives.

Lady Macbeth: But in them Nature's copy's not eterne.

Macbeth: There's comfort yet; they are assailable;
Then be thou jocund: ere the bat hath flown
His cloister'd flight, ere to black Hecate's summons
The shard-borne beetle with his drowsy hums
Hath rung night's yawning peal, there shall be done
A deed of dreadful note.
Lady Macbeth: What's to be done?
Macbeth: Be innocent of the knowledge, dearest chuck,
Till thou applaud the deed. Come, seeling Night,
Scarf up the tender eye of pitiful Day,
And with thy bloody and invisible hand,
Cancel and tear to pieces that great bond
Which keeps me pale! – Light thickens; and the crow
Makes wing to th'rooky wood;
Good things of day begin to droop and drowse;
While Night's black agents to their preys do rouse.
Thou marvell'st at my words: but hold thee still;
Things bad begun make strong themselves by ill.
So, prithee, go with me.
Exeunt *(432 words)*

Excerpt from: William Shakespeare: Macbeth, III, ii, v. 4–56, Reclam 1987.

Tasks

1. Briefly putting the scene into the context of the play, outline the state of mind Macbeth and his wife are in. *(12)*
2. Analyse the language used to convey Macbeth's and his wife's feelings at this point of the play. *(19)*
3. Discuss who is to blame for the murder: Macbeth, his wife or the witches. *(17)*

Lösungsvorschläge

Hörverstehen

Transkript: Fair is foul and foul is fair – Shakespeare's *Macbeth*

Neil MacGregor: I'm on Leith Pier near Edinburgh and I am standing on the spot where, historically, Scotland faced the world. For centuries Scottish ships set off from here, making the perilous journey across the North Sea to the European mainland and the wider world beyond.

In the autumn of 1589 a young Scot undertook this dangerous voyage, sailing from Leith to Norway and Denmark, and then back the following spring. The young man was the King of Scotland, James VI, and his ship was beset by such terrible storms that it nearly perished. James came to believe that the storms were more than just the usual bad Scottish weather. They were the work of evil Scottish witches.

All Witches: Double, double, toil and trouble;
Fire burn and cauldron bubble. (*Macbeth*, 4.1.35/36)

All: Fair is foul, and foul is fair.
Hover through the fog and filthy air. (*Macbeth*, 1.1.9/10)

Neil MacGregor: In Macbeth, Shakespeare opens the action by bringing us face to face with three extremely dangerous witches and throughout the play the "weird sisters" at their whim cause mayhem on land and sea. It was precisely this kind of witchly mayhem that led to the building of a finely crafted ship that was put on display in Leith in the late 16th century.

Today it's shown here, in the National Museum of Scotland. It's in fact a model ship, just 65 cm high. Made of wood, its hull is thickly painted in red and gold, and its figurehead is a boldly carved gold lion, and on the sides hefty white mermaids clutch their tails and sea gods wave their tridents.

At first glance you might think this model ship was a toy, but it was made not for the amusement of children, but as an offering to God. Ship models now usually serve as records of actual vessels but this one, it seems, was made to give thanks for survival at sea and for delivering the ship's passengers and cargo from the clutches of tempest-brewing witches.

For modern audiences it can be hard to grasp why Macbeth, a successful practical soldier, pays so much attention to what the witches tell him. But Shakespeare's public would most definitely have understood, for many of them, witchcraft was part of the fabric of daily life, as social historian Keith Thomas explains.

Keith Thomas: To ordinary villagers, labourers, small farmers, shopkeepers, witchcraft was the power to work physical effects by some supernatural occult means. Witches were divided into good witches, white witches, and bad ones, black witches. The good witches healed people by charms or prayers or some other form of mysterious activity. The black witches were people who did harm by occult means, typically by injuring people's animals, their livestock, or worse, by injuring or killing children, men or women.

First Witch: Where hast thou been, sister?

Second Witch: Killing swine. (*Macbeth*, 1.3.1/2)

Keith Thomas: And out of this there grew a huge literature of learned demonology which described how black witches flew through the air to black masses where they conducted obscene rituals, had sexual intercourse with the devil and, most important, made a contract with the devil. In other words, they were heretics. They had renounced God for the devil.

Macbeth: What is't you do?

Witches: A deed without a name? (*Macbeth*, 4.1.47/48)

Keith Thomas: The Reformation was immediately followed by witchcraft prosecution at a fairly intensive level, a concerted drive on the part of everyone, Catholics as well as Protestants, to complete the Christianisation of the population at large. And in the process, that sharpened the eye for any heresy – so people who turned to charmers and cunning folk, something had to be done about them. It was particularly the case in countries where the clergy were very influential: Scotland, a very good example of that.

Neil MacGregor: Scottish witches were, in one crucial respect, rather different from their English sisters. They were much more likely to be political, involved in high treason rather than local misfortune. Trying to sink the King's ship is exactly what you'd expect a Scottish witch to do. So, it's not at all surprising that in "the Scottish play" Shakespeare puts witches centre-stage, and in doing so he creates in *Macbeth* what becomes (and across the whole of the English-speaking world, still is) the definitive image of the witch. No Halloween night is now complete without some "secret, black, and midnight hags" stirring cauldrons and chanting spells.

All: Fair is foul, and foul is fair.
Hover through the fog and filthy air. (*Macbeth*, 1.1.9/10)

Neil MacGregor: Witches are by and large foul-weather friends. Macbeth's trio will meet in thunder, lightning and rain, but it never seems to occur to them to go out in the sun, and when they do go out they raise storms, flatten crops, scatter flocks and damage property, ships founder, lives are lost. They are "posters of the sea and land" making ports like Leith dangerously "tempest-tossed". Somebody has to be to blame for such things, especially for winds that can blow an anointed king off course, and that takes us back to our ship model. […] *(859 words)*

Hinweis: *When doing a listening test, the following tips might help you:*
- *Read the tasks carefully to be prepared for what is to come.*
- *In some items you will find words from the listening text. That does not necessarily mean that this item is the correct one.*
- *As you follow the listening text, follow the tasks. They are in chronological order.*
- *When listening for the first time, try to do as many tasks as possible.*
- *When listening for the second time, focus on the tasks you have not done yet.*
- *The last task requires you to prove your general understanding of the text. It is a*

good idea to answer this task after having listened for the second time.
- *Spelling and grammar are usually not assessed in listening tasks, but make sure that one can understand what you want to say.*
- *Even if you think that you have not understood much after listening for the first time, you will discover that you have grasped more than you think.*

1. Leith pier is the place where …
   - ☐ English ships set off on their perilous voyages.
   - ☑ Scottish ships embarked on their journeys.
   - ☐ the Scottish met people from all parts of Europe.
   - ☐ ships were built.
2. A young Scot started his voyage in **(the autumn of) 1589/autumn** and came back **the following spring**.
3. evil Scottish witches
4. The witches we encounter in Macbeth …
   - ☐ cause a restoration of power in Scotland.
   - ☐ fight chaos on land and sea.
   - ☐ solve people's problems.
   - ☑ trigger problems in all aspects of life.
5. 65 cm high / made of wood / its hull is painted in red and gold / its figurehead is a gold lion / on the sides, there are (white) mermaids/sea gods with tridents
6. This model ship …
   - ☐ shows evidence of Scottish inventiveness.
   - ☐ serves as a record of actual ships.
   - ☑ is a way to show a survivor's gratitude.
   - ☐ helps us to understand something about how to survive at sea.
7. part of (the fabric of) daily life
8. The social historian Keith Thomas explains that people at that time used witchcraft to …
   - ☑ understand the physical world.
   - ☐ effect a change.
   - ☐ grasp the supernatural.
   - ☐ recognise metaphysical workings.
9. charms/prayers/(some other form of) mysterious activity
10. injure people's animals (livestock)/injure (kill) children (men, women)

11. Because of the interest in evil spirits, many books were written about how …
- [ ] black masses were conducted.
- [ ] to become a witch.
- [x] witches renounced their pact with God.
- [ ] witches used their power.

12. they were prosecuted

13. Scottish witches are much more political (than English ones).

14. the image of the (stereotypical evil) witch was created

15. – to show the role of witches in Macbeth and
    – people's attitude towards witches in Shakespeare's time

Textaufgabe

1. ***Hinweis:*** *First explain why the scene takes place the way it does. Concentrate on the characters and actions that are important for this scene. Briefly explain its significance for the plot. Then focus on Macbeth's and Lady Macbeth's state of mind. If you have not read the play, focus on the second part of the task.*
   - *Putting the scene into the context of the play:*
     - *Macbeth and his friend Banquo: prophecies by three witches: Macbeth to become Thane of Cawdor and later King of Scotland. His children will not be kings; this honor is reserved for Banquo's sons. The first part of the prophecy instantly comes true.*
     - *Macbeth: letter to his wife, informing her of the prophecy and King Duncan's plan to visit their castle. She plots to kill the king, persuading her husband to go along with the plan.*
     - *Together they kill King Duncan. Duncan's sons flee the scene of the crime, Macbeth becomes King of Scotland.*
     - *To secure his power, Macbeth orders the murder of Scottish noblemen; at the same time, he and his wife begin to break down due to the mental strain.*
   - *Lady Macbeth's state of mind:*
     - *At the beginning of the scene she is the one in charge: calming her husband and telling him how to behave.*
     - *Although she at first seems to be at ease with the deed she has committed, she grows more and more quiet.*

     Macbeth's state of mind:
     - *At the beginning of the scene Macbeth seems to be struggling with the consequences of his deed.*
     - *At the end he takes the lead, ordering Lady Macbeth as to how to behave. He also conceals from her the fact that he has already ordered the murder of Banquo → complete reversal of roles.*

The excerpt from Act III, Scene 2 in Shakespeare's play *Macbeth* deals with the changing relationship between Macbeth and his wife after they have committed the regicide.
Macbeth, a Scottish nobleman, and his friend Banquo have received prophecies by three witches: Macbeth will first become Thane of Cawdor and later King of Scotland. His sons will not be kings, as this honour is reserved for Banquo's sons. When the first part of the prophecy instantly comes true, Macbeth writes a letter to his wife, informing her of the prophecy and King Duncan's plan to visit their castle. Lady Macbeth plots to kill the king and persuades her husband to execute the deed when he wants to stop it. After the murder has been discovered, Duncan's sons flee the scene of the crime for fear of being accused of patricide. Macbeth becomes King of Scotland. To secure his power, he orders the murder not only of Banquo but also of several Scottish noblemen. At the same time, he and his wife begin to break down due to the mental strain of the regicide.
At the beginning of this scene Lady Macbeth appears to be calm and reassured. She is the one in charge, calms Macbeth when he is agitated and confused and tells him how to behave towards his guests. Although she at first seems to be at ease with the deed she has committed, she grows more and more quiet.
Macbeth, on the other hand, first seems to be unsure: he is torn between remorse and euphoria and struggles with the consequences of his deed. However, his state of mind changes in the course of the scene; at the end of the extract he takes the lead and orders Lady Macbeth as to how to behave. He even conceals from her the fact that he has already ordered the murder of his friend Banquo.
All in all, it can be concluded that in this scene the audience witnesses a complete reversal of roles between the two partners in crime. *(339 words)*

2. ***Hinweis:*** *In this task, use your findings from task 1. Again, work on one character first and then on the other. Write an introduction in which you point out what your analysis is aimed at, and a conclusion in which you summarise your results – if possible with reference to your introduction. It is not necessary for you to analyse every detail of the excerpt. It is sufficient to outline the way Macbeth's and his wife's feelings are conveyed by giving evidence from the text.*
   - *Lady Macbeth*
     - *use of antitheses: "desire" – "(without) content" / "destroy" – "joy" (ll. 3–5).*
     - *giving her husband instructions on how to behave → imperatives: "(…), sleek o'er your rugged looks; Be bright and jovial among your guests to-night" (ll. 27/28)*
     - *One more order: "You must leave this." (l. 36)*
   - *Macbeth*
     - *Realising that the murder of Duncan is only the first in a long line → metaphor of the snake they have only wounded → "We have scotch'd the snake, not kill'd it:" (l. 12).*
     - *Not only is the "snake" not defeated, it also poisons him and his wife from*

within → "danger of her former tooth" (l. 14).

- *Emphasis on the fact that they are both responsible for the deed: "We" (l. 12), "our" (l. 13).*
- *Change in his view introduced by "But" (l. 15) → not worrying about the consequences of the murder on the divine and earthly order of things: "But let the frame of things disjoint, both the worlds suffer" (l. 15).*
- *However, inner conflict is underlined by antithesis: "Whom we, to gain our peace, have sent to peace" (l. 19); emphasised by an enumeration: "nor steel, nor poison, Malice domestic, foreign levy, (...)" (ll. 23/24).*
- *With regard to Banquo: pretending to be friends → metaphor "make our faces vizards to our hearts, Disguising what they are" (ll. 34/35).*
- *Last part: elaborate metaphor/allegory: The night – directly addressed – "Scarf[s] up the tender eye of pitiful Day" (l. 49), i.e. covers up all bad deeds; Macbeth calling the night to take him into its "dark side", enabling him to commit even more crimes: "While Night's black agents to their preys do rouse" (l. 55).*
- *Macbeth shelters his wife from his plans ("Be innocent of the knowledge", l. 47) tenderly calling her "dearest chuck" (l. 47) but hopes for her approval (l. 58).*

→ *Both Macbeth and Lady Macbeth: undergoing fundamental changes, former roles being reversed.*

In the excerpt from Act III, Scene 2 it becomes clear that both Macbeth's and Lady Macbeth's states of mind have undergone a fundamental change as concerns their attitude towards the regicide. This also becomes evident in the language they both use.

At the beginning of the scene (ll. 1–5), Lady Macbeth is alone. In contrast to previous scenes, where she is portrayed as an active, unscrupulous woman, she is now lost in thought, and ponders the consequences the deed has for her husband and herself. This change in attitude becomes obvious by the use of the antitheses "desire" – "(without) content"/"destroy – joy" (ll. 3–5), which illustrate her inner conflict. When her husband enters, she tries to conceal her doubts and to appear as determined as ever. She even advises her husband not to think about the deed when she tells him: "Using those thoughts which should indeed have died / With them they think on?" (ll. 9/10). She (desperately) tries to keep her position as the dominant partner when she gives her husband instructions on how to behave, using two imperatives: "(...), sleek o'er your rugged looks, Be bright and jovial among your guests to-night" (ll. 27/28), and even commands "You must leave this" (l. 36), but more and more, it becomes obvious that Macbeth has taken over her role of plotting and planning. Finally, there is nothing for her to do but ask: "What's to be done?" (l. 46).

When Macbeth enters the scene, he appears to be his old self, full of doubts and remorse, but he quickly begins to reassess the murder when he realises that the murder of Duncan was only the first in a long line of murders to come. He illustrates this new insight with the help of the elaborate metaphor of a snake: "We have

scotch'd the snake, not kill'd it" (l. 12). Comparing the murder of King Duncan to that of a snake – a lowly animal with very negative connotations – underlines Macbeth's new attitude towards Duncan: The murder of the (rightful) king is now akin to the killing of an animal. He goes on executing this metaphor when he says that the "snake" also poisons him and his wife from within: "danger of her former tooth" (l. 14). Using first person plural pronouns, Macbeth puts emphasis on the fact that both he and his wife are responsible for the deed.
When Macbeth introduces the next sentence with the conjunction "But" (l. 15), a certain change in attitude becomes obvious: He does not seem to worry about the consequences the murder has on the divine and earthly order of things: "But let the frame of things disjoint, both the worlds suffer" (l. 15). Simultaneously, Macbeth is afraid of not being able to sleep any more. His inner conflict is underlined by the antithesis "Whom we, to gain our peace, have sent to peace" (l. 19). In this context, he even envies Duncan, who can – finally – "sleep" well: "Duncan is in his grave; After life's fitful fever he sleeps well" (ll. 21/22), making the murder sound as if Macbeth has put Duncan out of his misery. This aspect is emphasised by the enumeration "nor steel, nor poison, Malice domestic, foreign levy, nothing Can touch him further" (ll. 23/24).
In the course of the dialogue, Macbeth extends his wife's rule of conduct, putting special emphasis on their behaviour towards their friend Banquo: they have to flatter him ("Present him eminence, both with eye and tongue: ... that we must lave our honours in these flattering streams" (ll. 32/33) and pretend to be friends still. The metaphor "make our faces vizards to our hearts, Disguising what they are" (ll. 34/35) underlines the aspect of pretence. Talking about Banquo, Macbeth hints at the fact that he is in their way and that "ere the bat hath flown" (l. 41) yet another "deed of dreadful note" (l. 45) will have been committed. It is noteworthy that Macbeth does not take his wife into his confidence about the plan he has already plotted.
The last part – starting in line 47 after Lady Macbeth has asked what needs to be done – is an elaborate metaphor: The night – directly addressed – "Scarf[s] up the tender eye of pitiful Day" (l. 49), i. e. covers up all bad deeds. Moreover, Macbeth calls the night to take him into its "dark side" to enable him to commit even more crimes: "While Night's black agents to their prey do rouse" (l. 55). Macbeth shelters his wife, who he tenderly calls "dearest chuck" (l. 47), from his new plans ("Be innocent of the knowledge", l. 47), but hopes for her approval: "So, prithee, go with me" (l. 58).
In conclusion, it can be said that both Lady Macbeth and Macbeth have undergone fundamental changes that reverse their former roles: Lady Macbeth from active, unscrupulous and demanding to thoughtful, passive and obedient; Macbeth from passive, hesitant, doubtful to energetic, unscrupulous and power-crazed. This change becomes visible in the way the characters speak about the crime and in their reassessment of what has been done and still needs to be done. Whereas Lady Macbeth speaks less and less, Macbeth takes over the role of the active part, speaking at greater length and using language that shows his growing brutality. *(887 words)*

3. ***Hinweis:** Here you have to discuss who is responsible for the murder of King Duncan. To come to a well-founded decision, collect aspects that speak for the guilt of each party and then assess whose responsibility weighs most. Start with the character/party that you consider less guilty and finish with the character that is most to blame for the regicide. If you have not read Macbeth in class, you can still answer the question with the help of the information in task 1 or with a synopsis of the play.*
   - *The three witches:*
     - *disclosing something that was already there (→ Macbeth's wish to become king).*
     - *Banquo's reaction to their prophecy serving as evidence for this thesis: not believing it from the start*
   - *Lady Macbeth:*
     - *instantly obsessed with the thought of becoming queen, ready to sacrifice everything to this obsession*
     - *willing to change her character, to get rid of her femininity*
     - *motivating, threatening and manipulating her husband*
     - *not executing the murder but planning it*
     - *after the murder, not involved in Macbeth's further killings*
   - *Macbeth:*
     - *witches' prophecies revealing latent wishes and desires*
     - *always wanted to take a place in the divine order of things that is not natural; as a member of the nobility: should know about his place in the chain of being and about the consequences of disturbing the divine order*
     - *being the one to execute the deed*
     - *Macbeth having been manipulated by the witches and his wife: might be considered in mitigation*
     - *but after the regicide: going on killing innocent people*

   → Macbeth can be seen as the main culprit whose latent desires and wishes have made him commit a crime against the divine order of things.

When considering who is to blame for the murder of King Duncan – Macbeth, his wife or the three witches – one should take a look at the extent to which each character is to blame. Only after a careful scrutiny of the evidence presented in the play is it possible to come to a verdict.

Although the three witches set off the tragedy when they prophesy to Macbeth that he will be king, they only disclosed a secret desire that was already in him. Otherwise their prophecy could not have worked on Macbeth that easily. Banquo's reaction to the witches' prophecy can serve as evidence for this thesis. Banquo did not believe the prophecy from the start, calling it nonsense. Moreover, the witches never told Macbeth when he will be king or even ordered him to commit murder.

Lady Macbeth is instantly obsessed with the idea of becoming queen when she reads of the prophecy in a letter her husband has written to her. She is more than ready to sacrifice everything to this obsession, willing to change her personality, offering to get rid of her femininity. Lady Macbeth even considers killing her own child if it were necessary. She motivates her husband when he is full of doubts and even

threatens to take her love away from him if he does not act according to his promise. Lady Macbeth plans the murder but does not execute it. The only aspect that speaks in her favour is the fact that she is not involved in the subsequent bloodbath.
That leaves Macbeth. It is more than obvious that the witches' prophecies have aroused latent wishes and desires, meaning that he has always wanted a place in the divine order of things – the chain of being – that has not been assigned to him. As a member of the nobility he must have known that such usurpation is unnatural and cannot succeed. Moreover, he is the one who executes the murder – according to his wife's plan. The fact that Macbeth has been manipulated by the witches and his wife might be considered in mitigation, but what speaks against this is the fact that he goes on killing innocent people after the regicide: his best friend Banquo, Macduff's family and many more. He is a tyrant who kills everyone who might be a danger to his reign.
In conclusion, it can be said that the three witches are not to blame as they did not tell Macbeth to kill King Duncan. Macbeth could have dismissed their prophecy as the "nonsense" of three weird ladies. Lady Macbeth is almost as guilty as her husband because she has plotted the crime and encourages him to go on with the deed when he has doubts. She is willing to do anything to become queen, but at least she seems to repent, fleeing into insanity. Therefore, Macbeth remains as the main culprit, whose thirst for power has made him commit a crime against the divine order of things. *(499 words)*

Sprechprüfung 1: Gun Control

Sprechprüfung 1: Gun Control (Einzelprüfung)

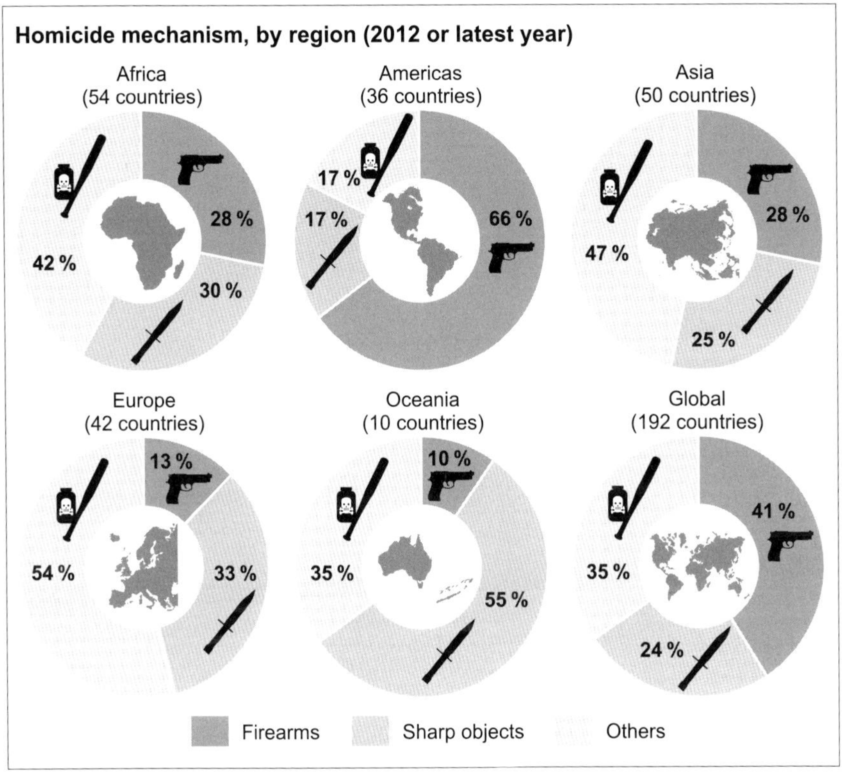

© *https://www.unodc.org/documents/gsh/pdfs/2014_GLOBAL_HOMICIDE_BOOK_web.pdf*

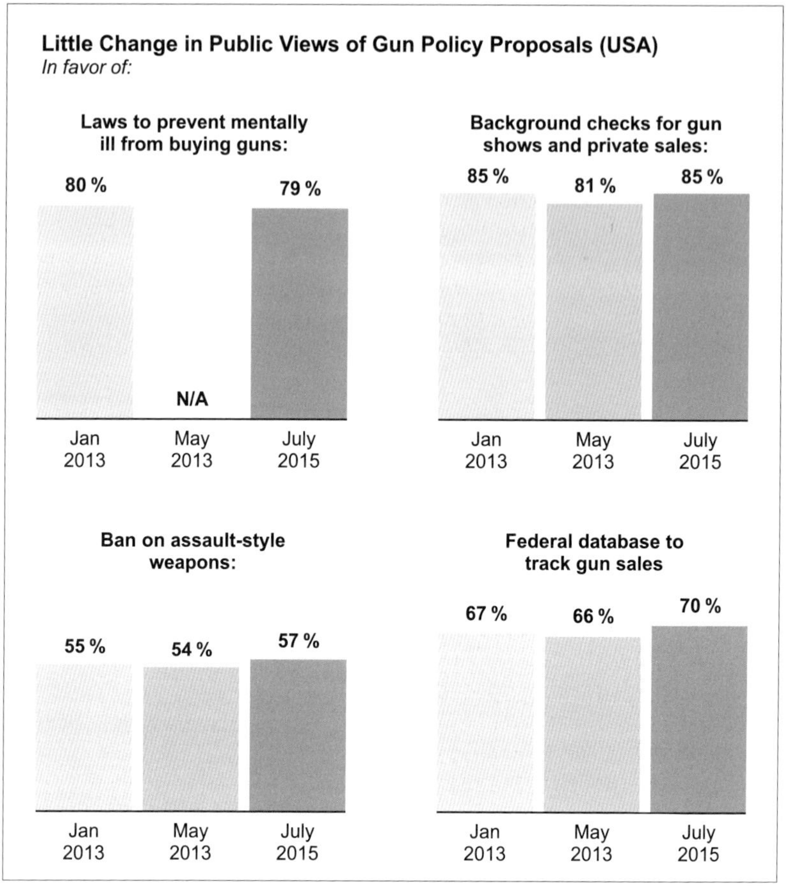

© *http://www.people-press.org/2015/08/13/continued-bipartisan-support-for-expanded-background-checks-on-gun-sales/pp_15-08-10_gunpolicy_640_social/*

Monologue

1. Analyse the graphs in the context of the current gun control debate in the United States.
2. Give reasons why guns play a prominent role in American society.

Dialogue

Discuss whether the US should introduce stricter gun laws.

Lösungsvorschläge

Hinweis: *This exam consists of two parts. The first part is a monologue based on the respective section on the worksheet. You need to be able to speak for five minutes and should plan your talk accordingly. Make sure that you present your topic coherently and do not just list facts.*
The second part is a dialogue based on the last task on your worksheet. You conduct the dialogue with your teacher, whom you should consider as an equal partner in this conversation. The dialogue lasts for 10 minutes. Make sure you listen actively and respond to the respective arguments rather than just naming one argument after another.
You have 15 minutes to prepare for this exam. You must not speak, but you should take notes (like in the following example solution), which you can use during the exam. You may use a dictionary.

Monologue

Example solution:

1. **Graph 1**
   - Six pie/donut charts showing the tools that are used to commit homicide (firearms, sharp object, others)
   - Each pie chart represents a continent and one pie chart summarises global data
   - Africa, Asia and Europe: roughly half of homicides committed with tools other than firearms and sharp objects
   - Oceania: majority of killings committed with sharp objects
   - the Americas (North and South America): difference to other parts of the world: two thirds of homicides committed with firearms.

   The graph shows that the use of firearms is a major problem on the American continent.

   Graph 2
   - Four bar charts showing public opinion on gun policy proposals from 2013 to 2015 in the USA
   - Most of the people asked favour stricter gun laws.
   - In 2015, 85 % favoured background checks for gun shows and private sales, 79 % approve of laws preventing mentally ill people from buying guns, 70 % are in favour of a federal database to track gun sales, 57 % want to ban assault-style weapons
   - Data rather stable, slight increase in favour of gun policy proposals between May 2013 and July 2015

   Despite stable and slightly increasing support for stricter gun laws, no major policy changes in the US: Trump administration unwilling to tighten the gun laws, rather suggesting teachers should carry weapons; however, as there is no end to shootings at US schools: an increasing number of students no longer willing to keep quiet and accept the status quo.

2. • 2nd Amendment (right to bear arms)
   • Tradition of self-reliance
   • History of Westward movement
   • Idea of liberty/ownership as liberty
   • Role of pressure groups (especially NRA)
   • Security issues in some parts of the USA

Dialogue

Discuss whether the US should introduce stricter gun laws.

Example solution:

Advocates of stricter gun laws:	Opponents of stricter gun laws:
• Large number of deaths related to gun violence • School shootings: killing of innocent children and teenagers • 2nd Amendment was relevant when the Constitution was written to form militias as the young state had no standing army; in the meantime: standing army and police: state should be able to make sure people can live in safety • Automatic weapons are much more dangerous than the arms the fathers of the Constitution knew • Majority in favour of stricter gun laws • Canada: despite similarities to the US (e. g. geography): different gun laws and fewer problems with gun-related crimes	• Right to gun ownership part of the founding documents of the US and American cultural heritage • In rural areas police often far away • Infringement of individual liberty rights • Gun industry provides jobs

Sprechprüfung 2: Science and Technology (Tandemprüfung)

Monologue: Partner A

Starting from the pictures, explain how technological innovations have affected or will affect people's lives.

Drohne: © Slavoljub Pantelic. Shutterstock, Auto: © Can Stock Photo/RioPatuca, Smartphones: © gpointstudio. 123rf.com

Dialogue

Discuss whether you agree or disagree with the following statement: "Scientists should be free to research and develop new technological advances without any constraint or restriction."

Monologue: Partner B

Starting from the pictures, analyse the positive and negative aspects of technological advancement.

MRT: © Image Source Trading Ltd. Shutterstock; Wissenschaftler: © endomedion. 123rf.com, E-Autos: © Sopotnicki. Shutterstock

Dialogue

Discuss whether you agree or disagree with the following statement:
"Scientists should be free to research and develop new technological advances without any constraint or restriction."

Lösungsvorschläge

Hinweis: *This exam consists of two parts. In the first part, each student gives a five-minute-talk based on the respective task on the worksheet. Since you need to be able to speak for five minutes without interruption, you should plan your talk accordingly. Make sure that you present your topic coherently and do not just list facts.*
The second part is a ten-minute-dialogue based on the second task on your worksheet. The two partners conduct the dialogue with each other; your teacher will only step in if you are stuck. Both partners should be equal in the conversation. Make sure you listen actively and respond to the respective arguments rather than just naming one argument after another.
You have 15 minutes to prepare for this exam. You must not speak to each other, but take notes (like in the following example solution), which you can use during the exam. You may use a dictionary.

Monologue: Partner A

Example solution:

Drones:
- surveillance of traffic, for example: smart controlling of traffic: fewer traffic jams
- delivery of packages, for example: would reduce number of delivery vehicles on the road
- warfare: highly controversial as innocent people can be killed

Self-driving vehicles:
- working or relaxing while driving
- as soon as the technology is perfected: fewer accidents as human error is eliminated

Mobile phones:
- multifunctional tools with apps for every area of life
- can be used everywhere
- make it easy to stay in touch with people
- however: many people "addicted" to their phones, neglecting personal communication

Monologue: Partner B

Example solution:

	Positive aspects	Negative aspects
Medicine	• more precise diagnoses • more effective treatment	• methods such as prenatal testing can create ethical dilemmas • some doctors overuse these methods to make profit
Genetic engineering	larger crop yields because of more resistant plants	• unforeseeable effects on people and environment • new breeds might drive out other species
Electric cars	more eco-friendly (less CO_2)	• battery production still not eco-friendly • cannot go long distances yet

Dialogue:

Discuss whether you agree or disagree with the following statement:
"Scientists should be free to research and develop new technological advances without any constraint or restriction."

Example solution:

Research without constraint	Research with constraint
• Strict rules for research and development hamper progress • Advances in medicine (e. g. antibiotics and vaccines) were also made because scientists were given freedom of research • Serious scientists know about their responsibility • Developments like global warming pose new challenges to humankind; science can help to meet these challenges	• Nuclear weapons show that science can be destructive • Ethically sensitive areas like stem cell research need a tight framework to prevent abuse • Throughout history, there have been scientists who abused their power, e. g. in Nazi Germany • Scientific development in certain areas has not undergone long-term studies, e. g. the effects of GM food on the human body and the environment